W. Watson Cheyne

Suppuration and Septic Diseases

Three Lectures Delivered at the Royal College of Surgeons of England in

February 1888

W. Watson Cheyne

Suppuration and Septic Diseases
Three Lectures Delivered at the Royal College of Surgeons of England in February 1888

ISBN/EAN: 9783337162962

Printed in Europe, USA, Canada, Australia, Japan

Cover: Foto ©Suzi / pixelio.de

More available books at **www.hansebooks.com**

SUPPURATION AND SEPTIC DISEASES.

SUPPURATION

AND

SEPTIC DISEASES

THREE LECTURES

DELIVERED AT THE ROYAL COLLEGE OF SURGEONS
OF ENGLAND IN FEBRUARY 1888

BY

W. WATSON CHEYNE, M.B., F.R.C.S.

HUNTERIAN PROFESSOR ; SURGEON TO KING'S COLLEGE HOSPITAL, AND TO THE
PADDINGTON GREEN CHILDREN'S HOSPITAL ; EXAMINER IN SURGERY AT
EDINBURGH UNIVERSITY.

EDINBURGH & LONDON:

YOUNG J. PENTLAND

1889

EDINBURGH: PRINTED FOR YOUNG J. PENTLAND BY SCOTT AND FERGUSON
AND BURNESS AND COMPANY, PRINTERS TO HER MAJESTY.

PREFACE.

IN reprinting these Lectures I have added a few notes where I thought that further facts might be of interest, but the Lectures themselves have not undergone any, or only a few verbal, alterations. In these Lectures my aim was not so much to detail original work—which is, I think, best given in special papers, in which the methods employed and the results obtained can be gone into in detail—as to summarise and give uniformity to the knowledge which has been gained by the work of many observers during the last few years. Of late years a certain antagonism has arisen between bacteriologists working in laboratories and clinical observers who do not possess a practical knowledge of bacteriology. The bacteriologist directing his attention mainly to the bacteria, has tended unduly to over-estimate the importance of these organisms; while the clinician, looking at the matter from the side of the body, has realised that an infective disease is a complex process, and has too often under-estimated the importance of the causal organisms. As one who has studied the subject from both points of view, though more from the clinical than the bacteriological side, I have naturally directed my efforts to the attempt to recon-

cile the apparently conflicting evidence, and in the present
Lectures I have tried to estimate, as fairly as I can, the
relative importance of the various factors which come into
play in the production of suppuration and septic diseases.
When all has been done we shall see how much we are still
in the dark as regards these processes; but it is only by
summing up our knowledge from time to time that we can
realise what we have gained, what are the points which most
urgently require elucidation, and what direction future investigations should take.

The history of this subject from the early publications
by Sir Joseph Lister down to the present time is one of very
great interest, as being the history of the groundwork of the
great revolution in Surgery of modern times, but it would
take up more space than I have at my disposal. I may,
however, indicate the three great landmarks in the development of our knowledge.

The first landmark of importance with regard to our
present views on this matter is the first papers by Sir Joseph
Lister on Antiseptic Surgery. At that time, and for some
years afterwards, little or nothing was known as to the
different species of micro-organisms and their different effects,
and consequently they were only spoken of in general terms.

Sir Joseph Lister's earliest views may be summed up as
follows :—It is the putrefaction of the discharges from a wound
that leads directly or indirectly to suppuration and septic
diseases; the causes of putrefaction are micro-organisms which
enter the wound from without, for—with a few rare exceptions,
such as osteomyelitis — suppuration does not follow injuries
where the skin remains unbroken and healthy; hence, an

essential part of the treatment of wounds must be to prevent the entrance of these organisms from without.

While the great majority of the cases treated on these principles supported his views, the absence of putrefaction and of suppuration and septic disease going hand in hand, cases every now and then occurred which led Sir Joseph Lister to see that this was probably not the whole truth. Thus, he found that the application of too much and too strong carbolic acid to a wound, instead of improving matters, was in some cases followed by suppuration. From this and similar observations he came to the conclusion that the irritation of the antiseptic itself, if sufficiently severe and long-continued, can cause suppuration. In other cases, again, he found that suppuration sometimes occurred when the discharge did not have free exit, and this he ascribed to nervous agencies brought into play by the tension thus excited. For these reasons he came somewhat later to the conclusion that there are three causes of suppuration in wounds, viz.:—(1) Suppuration from putrefaction of the discharges,—by far the most frequent and severe form; (2) suppuration caused by the antiseptic employed—"antiseptic suppuration"; and (3) suppuration from tension.

At this period, and for some time later, the view was still held that it was the *putrefaction* of the discharges, or rather the organisms which caused the putrefaction which led to the occurrence of suppuration; and the tests used to ascertain whether the antiseptic treatment had been successful or unsuccessful in its object, were—the smell of the discharge or dressings, the absence or presence of putrefactive odour, and, at a later period, the blackening of the protective where fermentation had occurred, due to the formation of sulphide of lead. Cases, however, occurred from time to time in which wounds suppurated without any reason for supposing that either tension or the irritation of the antiseptic were at work, and yet where there was no putrefactive odour and no blackening of the protective, and it thus became evident that in some cases, at any rate, the organisms which caused suppuration were not necessarily the same as those which caused putrefaction. It was the knowledge of this fact which led me, in my book on *Antiseptic Surgery*, to use the term " fermentation " of the discharges from the wound, rather than the word " putrefaction," for I assumed that all organisms cause some alteration, and most of them some fermentation, in the soil in which they grow, and thus I left the question as to the exact fermentative action of the pyogenic organisms undetermined.

Important observations then followed in Germany as to the presence of bacteria in wounds treated aseptically. These observations were, however, always open to the objection that the aseptic treatment had not been properly carried out ; but this objection was removed when, on examining wounds treated by Sir Joseph Lister, I found that in a certain number of them organisms were really present. I found that it was only, as a rule, when the dressings—carbolic gauze—had been left on for several days at a time that these organisms, which belong to the class of micrococci, made their appearance in the wounds. I have recently found that the organisms which usually appear are those forms of micrococci which are the most constant inhabitants of the surface of the skin, and which are non-parasitic. It was only in a few instances that the more hurtful forms entered, and in these cases their presence was generally indicated by suppuration, &c. Bacilli are never found in wounds covered with carbolic dressings, provided the treatment has been carried out properly. The entrance of these cocci can be avoided by frequent dressings, and by washing the skin over and beyond the whole extent of the dressings when changing them. They gain an entrance by growing in the discharge beneath the dressing, and so spreading into the wound, and also by growing in the superficial but dead layers of the epithelium, which protects them from the antiseptic in the gauze.

About this time (1879) observations were also being made as to the presence of micrococci in abscesses. Billroth found micrococci in a large portion of the acute abscesses which he examined, and Recklinghausen, Klebs, and others had often found micrococci in the pus of acute osteomyelitis. I found, by cultivation in cucumber infusion, micrococci in a certain, though small, proportion of cases, and for that reason I was inclined at the time to look on their presence as more or less accidental.

The second great landmark was the research by Professor A. Ogston, of Aberdeen, on micro-organisms in abscesses. This research threw a great deal of light on this matter, and Ogston's results are the basis of the more recent work on the organisms of suppuration. He examined the pus from a large number of abscesses microscopically, and found that micrococci were invariably present in acute abscesses, and in a few instances in certain situations bacilli were also found. Ogston further described two different kinds of cocci under the terms staphylococci and streptococci, according to the grouping of

the organisms, and he pointed out the frequent association
of the former with closed abscesses, and of the latter with
erysipelatous processes. He concluded from his experiment
that these cocci were the cause of the abscesses, and also that
erysipelas, pyæmia, and septicæmia, were the work of the
same organisms.

Ogston's statements were, in the main, soon confirmed by
a number of observers, and shortly afterwards Fehleisen demonstrated the streptococcus of erysipelas, and its causal relation
to that disease. Following on this, Loeffler and Becher
described a coccus (really the staphylococcus pyogenes aureus)
as the causal agent of acute osteomyelitis, and they were at
first inclined to regard it as a specific organism, and different
from those usually found in pus. This last conclusion, however, soon proved to be erroneous.

The third landmark is Rosenbach's work on the micro-
organisms in infective diseases of wounds, published in 1884,
a work which still forms the chief basis of our present knowledge of the subject. He demonstrated several different
varieties of pyogenic organisms, studied their characteristics,
and finally showed their causal connection with suppuration.
Rosenbach's work has been amply confirmed by subsequent
observers, and other pyogenic organisms have been found, and
many facts added with regard to their mode of action.

CONTENTS.

LECTURE I.

LECTURE II.

LECTURE III.

LIST OF ILLUSTRATIONS.

SUPPURATION AND SEPTIC DISEASES.

LECTURE I.

Introductory Remarks.—In studying the effects of pathogenic bacteria on animals, we frequently see great differences
between the effects of the same bacteria on different species of
animals, and even on the same species under varying conditions.
Inoculate guinea pigs with tubercle bacilli and we constantly
produce a rapid and general disease, which has little or no
tendency to remain localised, and no tendency to undergo
spontaneous cure; we are therefore naturally tempted to look
on the bacilli as the only noteworthy factor in the causation
of the disease, and to think that with the discovery of the
bacillus the etiology of the disease has been settled. On the
other hand, if we turn our attention to man, we see that
opportunities for infection with tubercle bacilli are frequently
present without being followed by infection; that the disease
assumes a variety of forms under a variety of external conditions; that it has comparatively little tendency to become
generalised; and that it has a strong tendency to cease either
spontaneously or under the influence of treatment not directed
immediately against the parasites. It cannot be a matter of
surprise if, under these circumstances, the clinical observer

A

concludes that the etiology of the disease has not been solved
by the discovery of the bacillus, or that he is inclined to regard
the organism as a very insignificant factor in its causation, or
even as a secondary, and perhaps unnecessary, accompaniment.
The fact is, however, that in these diseases we have two
opposing forces before us,—on the one side the bacteria, on the
other the body; and these forces are by no means always
equally matched; nor do they always bear the same relation
to each other in different species of animals. In some animals
the bacteria are more powerful than the body, the resistance on
the part of the body being scarcely, if at all, evident; in other
species of animals the same bacteria are much weaker than the
body, and if they succeed in entering the animal organism at all
they only do so by the aid of other conditions; and when these
conditions cease to act the bacteria again die out. In extreme
cases these conditions, by determining the seat and exact nature
of the resulting disease, are apt to give rise to the erroneous
belief that they are the essential ones.

This is well illustrated not only by the example given, but
also by the case of anthrax. Introduce a single anthrax
bacillus into a guinea pig and the animal dies with certainty
of a general disease, with only œdema at the seat of inoculation.
On the other hand, introduce anthrax bacilli into rats, and we
have a very different result, and one which varies according to
the age of the animal and the other conditions of the experiment. The result of the injection of a number of these bacilli
into a young rat, for example, is that the animal becomes very
ill, it may be, in some cases, even dies, while there is a production of sero-purulent fluid at the seat of inoculation. The older
the rat, up to a certain point, the less are the general symptoms
manifest, the thicker is the pus which is formed at the seat of
injection, and the sooner do the anthrax bacilli die out.

In spite of these different results we must none the less
admit that in each case the bacillus was the essential cause of
the disease, the difference in the characters of the disease being
due to differences in the strength of the opposing forces. In
the case of the guinea pig infected with anthrax, the bacillus is

so much more powerful than the body that the symptoms of resistance on the part of the latter are completely obscured. In the case of the rats, on the other hand, the opposing forces are more or less equal in strength, and, consequently, other conditions, such as age, seat of inoculation, &c., come into play and modify the character of the disease.

Duclaux, in his work, *Le Microbe et la Maladie,* mentions an excellent example of the part played by other factors in relation to infection. The itch of domestic animals is produced by an acarus which is almost visible to the naked eye ; it lives in the superficial layers of the skin. According to the experiments of Delafond and Bourgingnon, the acarus, when placed on the skin of well-nourished and healthy animals, cannot take root or form colonies. Sheep cannot be artificially inoculated with scab, but if they are first submitted to unsuitable conditions as regards nourishment and stabling, such as would debilitate them, the acarus can be very readily implanted, and it flourishes so long as the animals are kept in this unhealthy state. If, however, the nutrition of the animals is improved, if their stalls are cleaned and well aired, then, without any treatment against the acarus, the itch disappears and the animal becomes clean.

Another excellent example is that of *pebrine* and *flachérie,* pebrine attacking silk worms irrespective of their state of health or the existence of predisposition, and flachérie chiefly attacking worms whose digestive apparatus is weakened by previous disease or heredity.

In our surgical work we have to do with two diseases which illustrate in a very marked manner the action of the various conditions necessary for their production. These are : local tubercular affections, and suppuration with its allied diseases. I had at first intended to discuss both these diseases from this point of view, and such a discussion would have led to important deductions as regards treatment, especially in the case of the tubercular surgical affections; but when I came to put the material together, I found that it was far too great for the time at my disposal, and I therefore resolved to limit myself to a short sketch of the present state of our knowledge with regard to suppuration and septic diseases, with especial reference to the various conditions on the part of the body, and on that of the organisms, which are of importance in the commencement and continuance of these affections. And I may at once say that, as regards suppuration, I shall only refer to the acute form, the question of chronic suppuration being intimately bound up with that of surgical tubercular diseases, and differing greatly in its etiology and pathology from the other.

Description of the Pyogenic Organisms.—Before going into further details on this subject, it will be most convenient to glance briefly at the various organisms which have been found in association with acute suppuration. These organisms are distinguished from each other by their microscopical appearance, their characters on cultivation, and their effects on animals. The information obtained by means of the microscope is not much; in fact, beyond telling us whether we have to do with bacilli or with cocci, and whether we have to do with streptococci or staphylococci, the microscope does not aid us. In order to obtain more precise information it is necessary to employ various methods of cultivation, and, fortunately, as some of the organisms produce pigment while others do not, as some liquefy gelatine and others do not, and so on, we get further information of great value as regards the species present. In some cases also it is necessary to resort to the study of their effects on animals, in order to ascertain the existence of any differential characters between the organisms present.

1. Staphylococcus Pyogenes Aureus.

This is the organism most commonly present in acute suppuration. As the name implies the organisms are cocci,

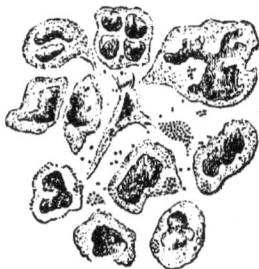

Fig. 1.—Staphylococcus Pyogenes Aureus (after Flügge).

which tend to arrange themselves in the form of bunches (Fig. 1). They grow readily at the ordinary summer temperature, but most rapidly above 30° C. When grown in gelatine they soon cause liquefaction of that medium, with the development of an orange-coloured deposit. When grown on agar kept at the body

temperature, we see, even after twenty-four hours, a whitish
or light yellow opaque layer at the point of inoculation, which
soon becomes more distinct, and of a bright orange yellow
colour. On potatoes it grows very readily, and presents the
same appearance. These organisms peptonise albumen very
energetically; they also give rise to a peculiar sweaty odour,
like that of decaying starch. They retain their vitality in
cultivations for a long time, and in the dry state they remain
alive for, at any rate, some weeks.

Injection of these organisms into animals gives varying
results, according to the number injected and the other conditions of the experiment; but, in the case of rabbits, it is
comparatively easy, on subcutaneous injection, to produce
suppuration; on intravenous injection, to set up abscesses in
the kidneys and also in other organs; and on injury to bone, to
cause suppuration in connection with the injured part. Injection of moderate quantities of the cultivations into the knee-
joints of rabbits usually causes acute inflammation with
suppuration, and ultimately the death of the animals; and in
the case of dogs, abscesses result, but not as a rule death.
This organism is the same as that described in acute osteo-
myelitis, and at first supposed to be the specific organism of
that disease.

2. STAPHYLOCOCCUS PYOGENES ALBUS.

This organism resembles the former in its conditions of life
outside the body, in the character of its cultivations, and in
its effects on animals, but it produces no pigment. As regards
its effects on animals, it is generally stated to be less virulent
than staphylococcus pyogenes aureus; but my own experience
is that, on the contrary, it is rather more virulent.

3. STAPHYLOCOCCUS PYOGENES CITREUS.

This organism, like the former, liquefies gelatine, and grows
both at the body and the summer temperature. After growing
for twenty-four hours on agar kept at the body temperature, the
cultivations present a light yellow colour, indistinguishable at

that period from cultivations of aureus; the latter, however, soon become darker, and orange yellow in colour, while citreus remains of a light yellow or citron colour. In both species the development of pigment only occurs where the colonies are in contact with air. The pathogenic properties of citreus are said by Passet to resemble those of aureus and albus, though it is not quite so virulent, abscesses following subcutaneous injection and injection into the knee-joint, while deposits in the kidney occur after injection into the veins. In my own experience these organisms have proved much less virulent than aureus or albus.

4. STREPTOCOCCUS PYOGENES.

These organisms are also cocci, which are arranged in chains often of great length (Fig. 2). They grow very slowly on the

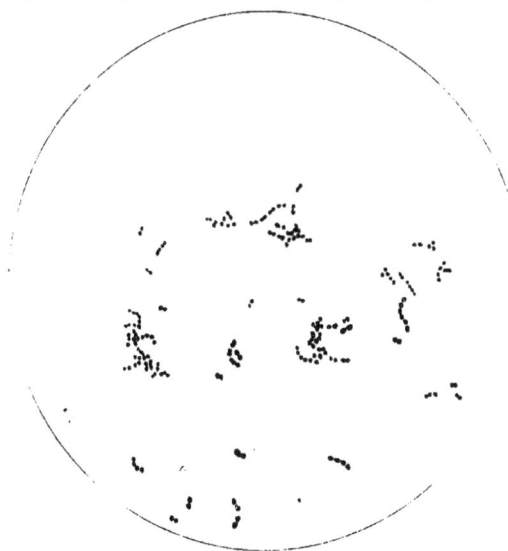

FIG. 2.—Streptococcus Pyogenes (from a photomicrograph, by Mr. Andrew Pringle).

ordinary culture media at the summer temperature, but with greater rapidity at the temperature of the body. On gelatine they form small colourless round colonies, but these do not spread to any appreciable extent on the surface of the gelatine. On agar kept at the body temperature, they have a tendency to grow in small points, which may attain the size of a pin's head; but, on the whole, the growth is very slow, and when sown on agar in the form of lines the growth does not, even after weeks, attain a greater breadth than two or three mm. They do not liquefy gelatine, but they exert an energetic peptonising action in the absence of oxygen.

When injected subcutaneously into rabbits, unless considerable numbers are introduced, the result is only a slight and transient redness; when larger quantities are employed, it is said by some authors that small circumscribed abscesses, resembling chronic abscesses, are formed. When injected into the knee-joint or into the pleura of rabbits, they at first cause slight inflammatory effusion, which however soon becomes absorbed without further bad consequences. Rosenbach was inclined to think that this organism differs from the form obtained by Fehleisen from cases of erysipelas, but that is a subject to which we shall presently allude.

When these streptococci are injected into the veins of rabbits after injury to the valves of the heart, endocarditis is set up. Loeffler isolated a streptococcus (*S. Articulorum*) in certain cases of diphtheria, which caused, when injected into the blood stream, suppuration in various joints ; and similar joint affections have been said to occur after injection of streptococcus pyogenes, but this observation is doubtful.

5. MICROCOCCUS PYOGENES TENUIS.

This species is of rare occurrence, in fact Rosenbach only met with it three times. On agar it forms an extremely delicate, almost invisible, layer. The individual cocci are irregular in shape, and larger than the preceding forms. No experiments have been made on animals.

6. ROSENBACH'S OVAL COCCUS.

Rosenbach found an oval coccus in one case of acute suppuration, which rapidly liquefies gelatine and causes suppuration when injected into the eyes of rabbits. This organism has not been further studied, nor has it as yet received a name.

7. Staphylococcus Cereus Albus.

This organism was found in abscesses by Passet. It forms a dull, white, wax-like layer on the surface of gelatine, and greyish white patches on potatoes. Its name is derived from the appearance of the growth on gelatine, on which the individual colonies look like drops of wax. It is not pathogenic in rabbits.

8. Staphylococcus Cereus Flavus.

This organism was also found by Passet, and closely resembles the former, with the exception that the cultivations have a beautiful citron yellow colour. It is not pathogenic in rabbits.

9. Passet's Pseudo-Pneumococcus.

Passet has also found an organism in the pus of acute abscesses, which closely resembles Friedlaender's pneumococcus. This organism forms greyish-white semi-circular elevations on the surface of gelatine, which may attain the size of pin heads. In the early stage of growth it is indistinguishable from Friedlaender's pneumococcus, but at a later period marked differences between the two can be made out, and that not only as regards the mode of growth, but also as regards the effects on animals. In the case of the pneumococcus, growth occurs not only on the surface of the jelly, but also along the entire length of the needle track; in the case of this organism growth occurs only at the surface, the organism being thus a typical aërobe. As regards the effects on animals, the pyogenic organism, when injected into the pleural cavity of mice and rabbits, causes pleuritis; and when injected subcutaneously, leads, in many instances, to the formation of abscesses in the same animals. On the other hand, Friedlaender's pneumococci are not pathogenic in rabbits.

10. Staphylococcus Flavescens.

This organism was found in an abscess by Babes, and occupies an intermediate position between aureus and albus. On nutrient jelly it forms a colourless layer, and liquefies the gelatine; on agar the growth becomes yellow after about eight days. It kills mice, sometimes causing abscesses, and sometimes, when in larger doses, septicaemia.

11. BACILLUS PYOGENES FŒTIDUS.

Passet found this organism in an abscess in the neighbourhood of the rectum. It is a bacillus which grows on nutrient jelly, forming a delicate white or greyish layer on the surface, but it does not liquefy the gelatine. Its growth on agar and potatoes has the appearance of a light brown glistening layer, which has a very foul smell; in milk this smell is not produced. Traces of the cultivation inoculated into mice do no harm; the injection of several drops causes septicaemia. Injection of about ten minims of an emulsion of the cultivation into a guinea pig caused an abscess in which the bacilli alone were found. The organism was not pathogenic in rabbits.

12. PNEUMONIA COCCUS.

In some cases of empyema occurring after acute pneumonia, the organism found in the pus is the pneumonia coccus described by A. Fraenkel, and regarded by him as by far the most frequent cause of pneumonia. On the other hand, in ordinary empyema, not in association with acute pneumonia, only the ordinary pyogenic cocci are present.

Other Organisms.—One or two other organisms have been described in acute abscesses, but as they are of no importance, I need not take up time in describing them.

13. GONOCOCCUS.

The gonococcus is constantly present in and is undoubtedly the cause of, acute gonorrhœa. The cocci occur in pairs or groups, the individuals not being completely spherical, but flattened on their opposed surfaces. This appearance was at first supposed to be characteristic of the gonococci, but of late it has been found that a number of other cocci, which grow rapidly, present the same character. In gonorrhœal pus the cocci are frequently present in numbers in the interior of the pus cells, and Bumm regards this arrangement as peculiar to these organisms. They have been cultivated outside the body, though with great difficulty; in fact, Bumm was not successful until he employed human blood serum. In this material the organisms form at the body temperature a delicate layer, which ceases to increase after about twenty-four hours, and must then be inoculated on fresh soil; they grow only on the surface of the serum. Bumm has definitely proved that this organism is causally connected with the disease by two observations on man, in one of which, the second generation grown on blood serum, in the other the twentieth generation, were introduced into the healthy female urethra, and caused typical acute gonorrhœa.

As this is a specific organism only occurring in gonorrhœal inflammations, it need not be considered further in these lectures; it may be mentioned, however, that in a certain number of cases the ordinary pyogenic cocci are also present in the pus from acute gonorrhœa, and that it is just in these cases that suppurative bubo occurs, the pus from the bubo containing the ordinary pyogenic organisms and not the gonococcus. Hence the occurrence of suppurative bubo in gonorrhœa is evidently accidental and due to mixed infection.

14. The Coccus of Erysipelas.

Although not a pyogenic organism this coccus must be shortly referred to. Micrococci have been observed by many investigators in the lymphatic vessels of the skin in cases of erysipelas, in largest numbers at and beyond the spreading margin of the redness, but Fehleisen was the first who succeeded in obtaining cultivations of these organisms, and in demonstrating their causal connection with the disease. As has just been said they are present in the lymphatic vessels at and beyond the margin of the redness, but in the parts where the redness is passing, or has passed off, the lymphatic vessels and the tissues in their neighbourhood become infiltrated with leucocytes, and the cocci rapidly die out. Fehleisen has succeeded in cultivating them on a number of media; on nutrient jelly they grow very slowly, and the individual colonies always remain small. They do not liquefy the gelatine, and the growth closely resembles that of streptococcus pyogenes.

If these organisms are inoculated on the ear of rabbits redness occurs, which spreads towards the root of the ear; and on making sections at the margin of the redness the lymphatic vessels are seen to be filled with the cocci as in man. Fehleisen has absolutely proved that these organisms are the cause of erysipelas in man, by inoculating persons, the subject of incurable tumours, with pure cultivations of the cocci. Of seven individuals so inoculated six developed typical erysipelas; in the seventh case the patient had suffered from an attack of erysipelas only a few weeks previously, and was, in all probability still protected from a fresh attack.

These inoculations may at first sight appear to be unjustifiable, but this is in reality not so, though they must not be undertaken unless there is a prospect of sufficient benefit from them to justify the risk incurred. It has more than once been observed and put on record that some forms of malignant tumours, too far advanced for operation, diminish considerably in size after an attack of erysipelas, and Busch has deliberately attempted to set up a curative erysipelas in such cases.

The details of Fehleisen's cases are interesting, and may be mentioned shortly. The method employed was to make superficial scarifications over the part, and then to rub in cultivations of the erysipelas coccus ; erysipelas followed in six out of seven cases, the incubation period varying from fifteen to sixty-one hours. Case I. was a patient suffering from multiple fibro-sarcomata of the skin. After the erysipelas had run its course there was a partial degeneration of the tumours, but the therapeutic result was not marked.—Case II. had been operated on thrice previously for cancer of the breast, and had a slight recurrence, but would not consent to further operation. The result in this case was the entire disappearance of the tumour after the erysipelas had passed off.—Case III. was one of very extensive sarcoma of the orbit and the glands at the side of the neck. The result was that, though no diminution occurred in the tumour, the glandular swellings shrank to less than half their original size.—Case IV. was a woman with extensive cancer of the breast, with numerous small nodules around the original tumour, Several of these nodules disappeared altogether, and a week after the cessation of the erysipelas the tumour was scarcely half its original size.—Case V. was a patient with extensive lupus of the face. The lupus healed as the result of the erysipelas, with the exception of a few nodules in the neighbourhood of the nostrils. These were afterwards scooped out, and up to the time at which Fehleisen published no relapse had occurred.—Case VI. was a woman with enlargement of the glands of the axilla and neck after a previous cancer of the breast. After the attack of erysipelas one of the tumours became soft and fluctuating, and ultimately discharged a white fluid.—Case VII. was a patient with lupus, who had previously had an attack of erysipelas, and in whom the inoculation was not successful. Cases have also been recorded by other observers,

in which erysipelas was set up by pure cultivations of these cocci, and in one or
two instances with fatal results.

Relation of Erysipelas Cocci to Streptococcus Pyogenes.—An
important question, and one which has been much discussed of
late, is the possible identity of these erysipelas cocci with the
ordinary streptococcus pyogenes ; in fact, a number of observers
now assert that the organisms are the same, and that the
different results depend on differences in the other conditions,
such as variations in virulence, dose, seat of inoculation, susceptibility of the host, &c. The earlier observers pointed out
certain distinctive characters between the cultivations of the
erysipelas organisms and those of the streptococcus pyogenes,
but closer examination and comparison of the mode of growth
of the two forms under similar conditions has failed to establish
any constant differences between the two.

In the case of animals, chiefly rabbits, the statements as to
the results of inoculation are very contradictory, for while some
observers seem to have been able to make out very definite
points of distinction, others have entirely failed to confirm their
results. Thus Hajeh states that the erysipelas cocci, when
inoculated into the ear of rabbits, cause a wandering inflammation, without any marked swelling at the seat of inoculation,
and that they chiefly inhabit the lymphatic vessels, and are
seldom found outside them ; while the streptococcus pyogenes,
inoculated in the same manner, causes wandering erysipelatous
inflammation and the production of an inflammatory swelling
at the seat of inoculation, and the cocci rapidly pass into the
tissue, being found especially in the neighbourhood of the blood
vessels, the walls of which they penetrate, and thus reach the
blood. Hoffa also has obtained results of a somewhat similar
character. He also notes that a doughy swelling, and ultimately
a large inflammatory tumour, developes at the seat of inoculation of the streptococcus pyogenes, while the erysipelas cocci
simply cause redness, without the development of any inflammatory tumour. On the other hand, several observers—Biondi,
Passet, Bumm, Von Eiselsberg, and others—have entirely failed

to establish any such differences in the effects on animals, and have come to regard these organisms as one and the same.

With reference to the attempt now being made to show that all these strepto-cocci in infective processes in man are the same, Hueppe has made an important observation with regard to a streptococcus, which he obtained from a case of puerperal fever. This organism formed typical arthrospores similar to those of *leuconostoc*, and did not grow in nutrient jelly, but grew well in blood serum. It was thus specifically different from the ordinary streptococci.

It is thus evident that the whole question is still *sub judice*. In any case these organisms are very closely allied, they are indeed probably varieties of the same species. But that we have to deal with absolutely the same organism, and that the differences in action do not depend on differences in their physiological characters, but simply on differences in the conditions under which they act, seems to me somewhat difficult of belief, and somewhat difficult to reconcile with clinical experience. It is quite possible, on the other hand, that two organisms may have the same microscopical characters, may grow in a similar manner in various culture media, and may have much the same effect on certain species of animals, and yet may not be the same; for when some other species of animal is tested, differences may be brought to light, the existence of which was not previously suspected. In proof of this, I need only refer to the example of chicken cholera, rabbit septicæmia, and swine fever, the organisms of which closely resemble each other, but apparently show differences when inoculated into certain species of animals. In the case of the organisms under discussion, it may quite well be that the differences between them are only brought clearly to light when they are inoculated on man.

As a matter of fact, in the cases where erysipelas has been produced in man by inoculation of pure cultivations only, organisms cultivated from cases of erysipelas have been employed, so that we have no absolute evidence as regards this matter; but there are facts which seem to show that inoculation of streptococcus pyogenes into the human skin does not cause erysipelas.

While there is no evidence that streptococcus pyogenes can produce erysipelas, it is asserted that the erysipelas cocci can cause suppuration. Thus, Hoffa obtained cultivations of what he considered to be erysipelas cocci from a case where suppuration occurred in the knee-joint beneath an erysipelas of the skin ; and he has also seen suppuration in the fossa above the clavicle, in a student, where an erysipelas of the head spread over this part. Of course the obvious objection here is that these were cases of mixed infection with erysipelas cocci and streptococcus pyogenes, and that what he took to be erysipelas cocci were, in reality, the pyogenic streptococci.

For example, streptococcus pyogenes is not unfrequently present in closed abscesses, and when these are opened the cutis is inoculated with the organisms; but so far as I am aware we have no evidence that erysipelas has ever resulted in such a case, or that a surgeon with a wound on his finger gets erysipelas from dabbling in pus containing streptococcus pyogenes. Rosenbach also mentions a fact which shows the action of streptococcus pyogenes on the human skin. He states that after opening an empyema which contained streptococcus pyogenes, a dense inflammatory induration, what was practically a boil, developed around the incision : erysipelas did not occur. Till, therefore, more definite evidence in favour of the unity of these organisms is produced than we at present possess, I am inclined to uphold the specific character of the coccus of erysipelas.

Occurrence of Pyogenic Organisms in Disease.—The diseases in which the pyogenic organisms occur are very various, in fact they are present practically in all affections accompanied by acute suppuration. Thus they are found in acute abscesses, boils, carbuncles, whitlows, spreading suppuration, acute osteo-myelitis, suppurative arthritis, suppurative peritonitis, empyema, ulcerative endocarditis, pyæmia, puerperal fever, the pustules of small-pox, etc.

Frequency of Occurrence of each Variety.—As regards the frequency of occurrence of the individual species, Zuckermann has put together the results obtained by a number of different observers in 495 abscesses, and he states that staphylococcus was present in 71 per cent. of the cases, streptococcus in 16 per cent., the two organisms together in 5·5 per cent., and the remaining pyogenic organisms only exceptionally. As regards the pyogenic cocci individually, in 172 cases in which definite statements are made, we find that staphylococcus pyogenes aureus occurred alone, or in combination with other staphylococci, 123 times; and that streptococcus pyogenes was present alone 35 times, and in combination with staphylococcus, 8 times. Staphylococcus pyogenes albus occurred alone 25 times in 133 cases, and in combination with aureus also 25 times. The other pyogenic organisms occur comparatively rarely; thus, citreus was only found 7 times in 133 cases—4 times alone, and 3 times in conjunction with other forms; staphylococcus cereus albus was found 3 times in the same number of cases, and staphylococcus cereus flavus only once. Micrococcus pyogenes tenuis was found 3 times by Rosenbach in 39 cases (2 of these were cases of empyema, and 1 a case of acute abscess); the organism described by Passet as closely resembling Friedlaender's pneumococcus, was found in 2 out of 33 cases (in 1 case in an ordinary acute abscess, and in the other in an acute abscess after pneumonia); and the bacillus pyogenes foetidus was only found on one occasion, viz., in an ischio rectal abscess.

Action of Staphylococcus and Streptococcus.—The organism, therefore, which occurs most frequently in these diseases is the staphylococcus pyogenes aureus, and the next in frequency is the staphylococcus pyogenes albus. Both are associated with closed acute abscesses, also with boils, acute osteo-myelitis, &c., and albus is apparently associated with somewhat more severe inflammations than aureus; the combination of the two, in acute osteo-myelitis for example, seems to be particularly unfavourable. The streptococcus pyogenes is also frequently present, but it is especially associated with phlegmonous and erysipelatous processes, where the pus occurs in the form of infiltration of the tissue, accompanied by death of portions of tissue. It also occurs, as pointed out by Ogston and Rosenbach, in progressive gangrene, and is the chief organism of pyaemia, having been present in five out of six cases examined by Rosenbach.

Mastitis in women offers a good example of the different

mode of action of these two species of pyogenic organisms. The abscesses in the mamma, which are caused by staphylococci, always begin in the deeper part of the organ and spread towards the surface, while in the case of the suppurations which occur in connection with streptococci the disease commences with a rapidly spreading redness of the skin, extending from some crack or fissure on the nipple, and the suppuration in the deeper parts follows this superficial affection. The explanation of these differences is that the staphylococcus usually spreads up the milk ducts and acts from their interior, whereas the streptococcus spreads along the lymphatic vessels, and its pathogenic action commences at the surface. This statement as to the action of the staphylococci from the interior of the ducts and acini, in the first instance, is not a mere theoretical deduction, for Bumm excised a portion of the wall of a commencing mammary abscess, and was able to demonstrate the presence of

Fig. 3.—Section of the wall of a commencing Mammary Abscess, showing the presence of Staphylococci in the interior of the ducts and their penetration into the tissue (after Bumm).

the cocci in the acini, and their penetration from thence into the interacinous cellular tissue (Fig. 3).

Kitt has specially investigated mastitis in cows, and has cultivated cocci from these cases differing from the cocci found in man ; the injection of these cocci set up suppurative inflammation. Thus, in one case, he injected pure cultivations of one of these species of cocci into the milk ducts, with the result that on the evening of the same day the corresponding quarter of the udder became swollen, and by the next day was hot, swollen, hard, and very painful ; the milk from that teat was yellow, turbid, and flaky, and contained pus cells.

These Organisms cause Suppuration.—We must now pass on to the evidence which leads us to believe that a causal connection exists between these pyogenic organisms and acute suppuration. In the first place they are constantly present in acute abscesses and in suppurations generally, and, as has just been pointed out, certain species are generally associated with certain types of inflammation; thus, the association of streptococci with spreading suppurations, and of staphylococci with circumscribed abscesses, being constant, can hardly be accidental.

Experiments on Animals.—Numerous experiments have been made on animals which show that these organisms, when introduced under suitable conditions, can set up suppuration, and I have previously mentioned some of their effects on animals. The conditions necessary for infection are very various, more especially as the animals usually employed for the experiments are not very susceptible to the action of these organisms, but I need not refer to these conditions at present.

Professor Schütz has demonstrated the causal connection of a pyogenic coccus with strangles in horses. This disease occurs under two forms. In both it usually begins as a catarrh of the mucous membrane of the nose, and in the milder form this is followed by swelling and suppuration of the glands in the neck, more especially of the submaxillary glands, and of the glands around the pharynx. In the severe form metastatic abscesses occur throughout the body; in fact, the animal dies of a disease corresponding in all respects with pyæmia. On examining the pus from these abscesses, whether in the mild or the severe form, Schütz found a streptococcus constantly present in the pus which presented special characters, and which differed from any of the organisms which I have mentioned as occurring in man. He cultivated these cocci outside the body on the blood serum of horses, and was able to reproduce the disease, in a foal, for example, by injecting some of the cultivation into the nasal cavity. As a result of the injection the nasal mucous membrane became swollen and inflamed, and the animal suffered from a muco-purulent catarrh; this was followed by swelling and suppuration of the submaxillary glands, the pus from the abscesses containing the same streptococci. These organisms also set up suppuration when injected subcutaneously into mice.

One experiment will suffice to show that these organisms can cause suppuration in rabbits. Knapp has performed a number of experiments in connection with the process of healing of wounds of the eye in rabbits. A similar operation was performed on both the eyes of the same animal; on the one eye

B

the operation was performed aseptically, the hands, instruments, &c., being carefully disinfected, and care being taken to exclude organisms during and after the operation, but no antiseptic was applied to the wounds: on the other eye the operation was performed in the same manner, but, after it was finished, the wound was infected with pyogenic cocci, usually with the staphylococcus pyogenes aureus. As a result, all the aseptic eyes, though very roughly handled, healed without a trace of suppuration, while almost all the other eyes were destroyed by suppuration, and only in those cases where the operation was superficial and not extensive did suppuration cease without complete destruction of the eye.

Experiments on Man.—Absolute proof of the causal connection of these organisms with suppurative diseases has been furnished by experiments on man, of which we have three kinds. We have, firstly, a considerable number of experiments where superficial abscesses have been induced by the introduction of organisms under the superficial layers of the epidermis; secondly, some where impetigo pustules, &c., have been caused by inunction of these organisms into the skin; and thirdly, experiments where abscesses have been caused in the subcutaneous tissue by subcutaneous injection of the organisms.

Superficial Inoculations.—As all the experiments in which superficial inoculations were made yielded similar results, it is unnecessary to mention more than one as an example. Take for instance one of Bockhardt's experiments:—He introduced a trace of the mixed cultivations of aureus and albus into the cutis of his left forefinger; after forty-eight hours an abscess, the size of a small lentil, had formed and was opened, and the pus contained staphylococcus pyogenes aureus.

Inunction.—Garré's case of inunction of a cultivation of staphylococcus pyogenes aureus into the skin is probably well known, but I may mention it for the sake of completeness. He thoroughly cleansed the skin of his left fore-arm with distilled water, and taking a cultivation of aureus in gelatine, rubbed it well into the arm in the same manner as one would rub an ointment into the skin. For purposes of control, he rubbed a small quantity of sterilised agar jelly into the skin of his right fore-arm in the same manner, and it was noted that there was no wound or pustule on either arm. It may be said at once that the result on the control arm was *nil.* In the case of the other, a burning sensation began at the seat of inunction six hours later; this burning sensation became more intense, redness and swelling developed, and on the evening of the same day a number of pustules, the size of a pin's head, appeared, especially in connection with the hairs. On the following day these pustules had attained the size of a lentil, contained a small quantity of pus, and were surrounded by an inflammatory area. The inflammation increased in intensity, and on the fourth day the seat of inunction presented the appearance of an enormous carbuncle surrounded by a ring of pustules. Ultimately, more than twenty openings formed, discharging pus and portions of dead tissue.

Bockhardt performed somewhat similar experiments on himself, inoculating in the same manner a portion of the skin of his forearm, about the size of a five shilling piece, the part having been cleansed and disinfected, and slightly scraped in places with his finger nail. The organisms used were a mixture of staphylococcus pyogenes aureus and albus. This mixture was rubbed into the arm at 4 p.m.; at 10 p.m., that is to say, six hours later, the seat of inoculation was slightly reddened and somewhat painful; fourteen hours after infection there were, at the seat of inoculation, twenty-five closely aggregated impetigo pustules, varying from the size of a pin's head to that of a lentil, a few, but not the majority of these, being traversed by hairs. These pustules contained the cocci employed, and by about the sixth day they had dried up and disappeared. Some days later a similar experiment was performed with the same mixture. The inoculation took place at six in the evening, the cultivation, mixed with sterilised salt solution, being rubbed into the outer part of the forearm. Next morning at 6 a.m. the seat of inunction was covered partly with impetigo pustules, of which he counted thirty-five, and partly with small slightly red patches; between 6 and 11 a.m. he saw twenty-five impetigo pustules form on these red patches before his eyes, most of these pustules being perforated by hairs. After eight days most of the pustules had dried up and disappeared, except two which had developed into large and painful boils, and for the next two

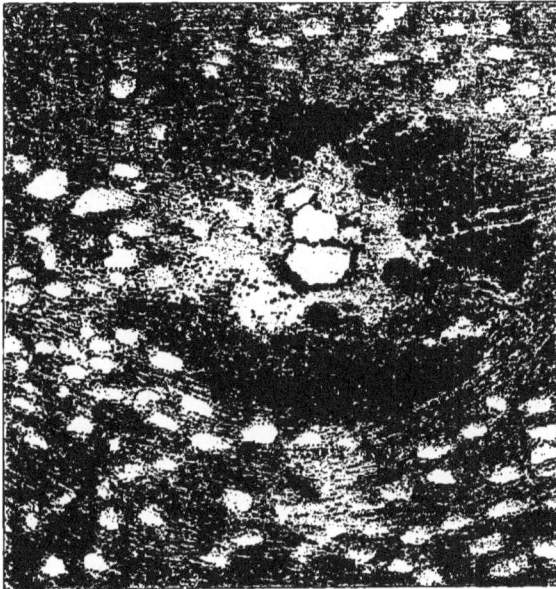

FIG. 4.—Section of the kidney of a rabbit, showing a central mass of micrococci surrounded by a clear necrotic area, and further out by a ring of leucocytes. (From a photo-micrograph by the author.)

or three months he was subject to a recurrence of impetigo pustules on the skin of his left forearm. As will be evident, the results in Bockhardt's cases were milder than in Garré's, and Baumgarten attributes this, and probably correctly, to the fact that Bockhardt rubbed in a much more dilute mixture of the organisms, and also a smaller quantity of them. That this may quite well account for the differences will be evident when we come to consider the question of the dose of organisms.

Bockhardt defines impetigo after Wilson as a pustular eruption, which appears at once as pustules on the skin, not being preceded by nodules or vesicles. These pustules appear suddenly, are generally small and do not enlarge, soon dry up and form crusts, have often a hair in their middle, and the skin in their vicinity is not altered, or only slightly reddened. They may occur anywhere except where there is much hair; in such situations, Bockhardt thinks that if the same cause acts, sycosis will result. In Wilson's impetigo he has always found staphylococcus pyogenes aureus and albus, and the same organisms are present in boils; in fact, Bockhardt holds that the impetigo pustule is often a forerunner of a boil, for it is often situated on and precedes it.

Experiments have also been performed by Zuckermann with similar results.

Subcutaneous Injection.—Bumm injected pure cultivations of what was apparently staphylococcus pyogenes aureus into the subcutaneous tissue of his own arm, and into the arms of two other persons. The cultivations were mixed with a few drops of salt solution before injection. On each occasion an abscess developed, which varied from the size of a pigeon's egg to that of a man's fist, according to the time which elapsed before it was opened, and these abscesses contained large numbers of the organisms employed.

Anatomy of Abscess.—As regards the mode in which an abscess is produced by these organisms, a considerable number of facts have recently been obtained from the examination of parts after infection. Where the organisms are circulating in the blood, and become deposited in the smaller capillaries in the form of plugs, as is seen in pyæmia, the first effect is the change in the tissues, termed by Weigert "coagulation necrosis," and figured by me in a paper on "Micrococci in relation to Wounds, &c.," published some years ago (Fig. 4). On staining sections of tissue in which these plugs are present with the ordinary aniline dyes, it is found that, while the mass of organisms is intensely stained, and while the nuclei in the greater part of the section have become well coloured, there is a ring of tissue around the central mass of organisms which does not take on the stain, and which presents a homogeneous translucent appearance; this ring evidently results from the action of the concentrated products of the micrococci, the tissue being brought into the condition of coagulation necrosis. After some hours a second ring appears at a greater distance from the mass of organisms, this ring, being

composed of a dense layer of leucocytes, apparently collecting
where the chemical substances are more dilute, and do not
interfere with the life of the cells.   As time goes on, the intermediate translucent layer becomes infiltrated on the one hand
with cocci from the central plug, and on the other hand with
cells from the outer ring; and the original tissue rapidly
disappears, probably in part as the result of the peptonising
action of the cocci.   At the same time the fluid effused does not
coagulate, probably also on account of the peptonising action of
the cocci on the fibrinogen, and thus we come to have a central
collection of fluid containing leucocytes and micrococci, surrounded by a wall of leucocytes and cocci—in other words, an
abscess.

When the cocci spread into the surrounding tissue after
injection, from wounds in the skin, etc., they apparently at
first frequently follow the course of the lymph channels.   In
the case of injections, as in Bumm's cases, we find at the seat
of injection a central mass presenting a yellowish appearance,
due to the presence of large numbers of leucocytes and cocci
infiltrating the injured parts, this central yellow mass being
surrounded by an inflamed area in which are also leucocytes
and micrococci.   At the margin of the inflamed area the cocci
are seen to be multiplying and penetrating into the surrounding
tissue in all directions, the mode in which they spread varying
according to the density of the tissue; thus where the tissue
is fairly dense, they spread in masses, while in the loose tissue
they form small groups and chains of four to six members.
The cellular tissue attached soon loses its fibrous appearance,
the fibrillæ swelling up and a homogeneous mass forming, this
mass ultimately undergoing liquefaction just as in the case
previously described.   Beyond the area of infiltration with
organisms, a layer of leucocytes is formed, but at first this layer
does not seem to be able to oppose the spread of the organisms.
In rabbits, however, after about the third, and more especially
the fourth day, their spread begins to be limited, and the zone
in which the cocci are penetrating into the tissue becomes
thinner.   In rabbits, by the ninth day, the tissues have, as a

rule, completely got the upper hand, and the micrococcal growth is surrounded and limited on all sides by a layer of leucocytes.

In the case of Proteus vulgaris, which causes abscesses in rabbits, and of the bacillus of chicken cholera, which causes abscesses in guinea pigs, there is usually a mass of necrotic tissue in the interior of the abscess, possibly left undissolved on account of their feeble peptonising power.

The sequence of events in man is quite similar, but, as a rule, the cocci become enclosed more quickly than in rabbits.—I should say that I have been speaking here of the effects of the staphylococci; the mode of spread and action of the streptococci is, as Ogston first pointed out, and as will be afterwards mentioned, somewhat different, and apparently the differences bear some relation to the differences in peptonising power of these two species of organisms.

As regards the mode in which the cocci act on the skin, for example in the experiments made by Bockhardt, the following seem to be the facts. The points at which the pyogenic cocci penetrate into the skin, are the ducts of the sweat glands, the orifices of the sebaceous glands and hair follicles, and portions of the skin where the protective epidermis has been scratched or destroyed. If micrococci penetrate by one or other of these paths into the skin, they multiply either in the wall of the ducts of the sweat glands and the adjacent part of the Malpighian layer, or they penetrate into the external root sheath and into the Malpighian layer at the orifice of the hair follicles, or they develop at some part of the Malpighian layer which has been deprived of its epidermic covering. They multiply rapidly at the seat of infection, and set up violent suppurative inflammation in the neighbouring papillæ. The violence of this inflammation is evident from the rapidity with which the pustules appear after inunction. As a rule, when the micrococci only set up impetigo pustules, they do not spread beyond the epidermic tissue; if they do so, we have the conditions necessary for the production of an abscess in the skin. This, however, generally only occurs after coarse mechanical injury to the skin. A boil developes especially from the impetigo pustules which have formed in connection with the hair follicles or with the orifices of the ducts of the sweat glands. After the micrococci have entered these parts and set up the impetigo pustules, they gradually spread in the wall of the ducts until they reach the end of the sweat gland or sebaceous or hair follicle. Coagulation necrosis occurs around them, and violent inflammation is set up in the vascular tissue surrounding these ducts and glands, with the result that a layer of leucocytes is formed like a wall around the affected epithelial tissue. As the necrosed wall of the duct or hair follicle becomes infiltrated with pus cells, the core of the boil is formed, pus collects around the core, and ultimately the skin gives way and it is expelled.

Can suppuration occur without micro-organisms ?—Although it is thus evident that these organisms can cause suppuration, a very important question, and one which has been much debated, still remains for consideration, viz., whether suppuration can occur without the action of micro-organisms.

Absence of Organisms in acute Abscesses.—It is only in a very few instances that pyogenic organisms have been missed in acute abscesses. In two cases of suppurating hydatid cysts, Rosenbach did not see any organisms, but they have since been found in a number of similar cases which have been examined. In cases of suppurating bubo after soft chancres, organisms have not been found in a considerable number of instances, especially in those which become chancrous surfaces after being opened, while in other cases the ordinary pyogenic cocci have been present. In the former case, however, the abscess is without doubt caused by the virus of soft chancre, a virus which is in all probability of a bacterial nature, but which has not as yet been satisfactorily demonstrated. As this is the case, it can hardly be a matter of surprise that organisms have 'not been found in a certain proportion of these buboes, and that, under certain circumstances, pyogenic organisms are present is only what we should expect as the result of the mixed infection which is so apt to occur. Although, therefore, organisms have not been found in some of these cases, we cannot conclude that none are present. With these exceptions, we always find that acute suppurations, occurring naturally, are associated with the pyogenic micro-organisms.

De Luca states that he has isolated very small cocci which produce soft chancres, and which he looks on as the virus of the disease. This *micrococcus ulceris* is a typical aërobe, and he explains the fact that these buboes are not infective till two or three days after they have been opened, by supposing that it is not till the access of air has been permitted for two or three days that the organism attains its full activity. If this be so, it is an argument against free incision into these buboes.

Experiments on Animals.—Numerous experiments have been made to see whether it is possible that suppuration can occur as the result of injuries of a mechanical or chemical nature without the intervention of micro-organisms. As a result it may be regarded as settled, in the case of the lower animals at any rate, that mechanical injuries, though frequently repeated, cannot of themselves cause suppuration ; and, as a matter of fact, the whole discussion at the present time is limited to the effect of a few acrid chemical substances, viz., croton oil, ammonia, and oil of turpentine.

With regard to these substances, a great number of investigations have been made with contradictory results. On the one hand, a number of observers state that one or all of these substances can cause suppuration in animals. I myself came to the conclusion some years ago that croton oil could cause suppuration in rabbits. Omitting the earlier experiments, which were not free from objection, I may mention the method which I ultimately adopted, with the view of excluding all possible contamination with micro-organisms. I took a mixture of equal parts of croton oil and olive oil, sterilised it, introduced it into sterilised glass capsules, which were then sealed at both ends. An incision was made antiseptically in the muscles of the back of a rabbit, and the tube introduced into the muscles ; the wound was then stitched with catgut, and an antiseptic dressing applied. The result was, that in a certain number of cases the wound healed by first intention, and the glass capsule remained imbedded in the tissues as an unirritating foreign body. After a certain time had elapsed, the capsule was broken by slight pressure against the spine, and thus the croton oil was brought into contact with the tissues. In one experiment performed in this way the tube was broken fifty-four days after its insertion, and the animal was killed twenty-seven days later. On making an incision into the part, a quantity of putty-like material was found. In another experiment, forty-five days elapsed between the operation and the breaking of the tube, and the result was the same, except that there was a much smaller quantity of this putty-like material. No organisms were present in either case. Councilman and others who have followed the same plan mention similar results, as do also other observers, such as Orthmann, Grawitz, and de Bary, &c., who have adopted different methods.

Curiously enough Councilman and I adopted exactly the same method independently of each other. Councilman published his experiments before I did, but mine were done some months before his. I performed several preliminary experiments with goldbeaters' skin, &c., before I took to the glass capsules; and the reason why I diluted the croton oil with olive oil was, that I found that if I used the pure croton oil, the animals were apt to die of poisoning a few hours after the tube was broken.

Orthmann states that he has caused suppuration in dogs by the injection of considerable quantities of turpentine oil into the tissues, and that in none of the cases could micro-organisms be found, either microscopically or by cultivation.

Grawitz and de Bary also state that turpentine causes suppuration in dogs, and that large quantities of ammonia do the same. These experiments, however, require careful repetition.

On the other hand, we have a number of experiments carefully conducted by a number of independent observers, in which no suppuration has followed the introduction of irritating chemical substances. Thus Straus took especial care that organisms should not be introduced along with the material injected, by cauterising the surface of the skin at the seat of injection, so as to destroy the organisms on it, and he is positive that these substances do not cause true acute suppuration. Perhaps the most valuable of these researches is that by Klemperer, who adopted Straus' method with still greater precautions. He states that he has failed to cause true suppuration by the injection of these substances, except in cases where micro-organisms were present at the same time. I may also mention a research by Ruijs, where the materials were injected into the anterior chamber of the eye, and where the effect could be watched. Here also it was found that if organisms are absent, suppuration does not follow the introduction of these chemical substances.

Christmas (*Annales de l'Institut Pasteur*, 1888, No. 9, p. 469) comes to the conclusion that turpentine does not cause suppuration in rabbits, but that it does do so in dogs.

While it is a question how far we can look on this matter as quite settled, it is clear that in weighing the evidence most stress must be laid on the negative results. If a number of careful observers have entirely failed to produce suppuration by the injection of these irritating chemical substances, then those who have obtained a contrary result must either have brought some other factor unwittingly into play, or there must be some other explanation of the results.

The explanation of the positive results given by those who hold the opposite view is that organisms were really present in the pus, but were either missed from imperfect examination, or had died out before the abscess was opened. Speaking of my own results, I am positive that organisms were not present in a living state, and though it is quite possible that they may have been present at an earlier period, and have died out before I opened the part, I do not think that this is a satisfactory explanation, for other observers have examined the seat of injection at an earlier period than I did, and have likewise failed to find micro-organisms. Besides, the character of the disease induced is different from that caused by micro-organisms ; in the latter case we have a progressive suppuration, an abscess which goes on spreading, whereas those who speak of suppuration occurring after the introduction of croton oil, etc., state that it is not a progressive suppuration, and does not resemble that caused by micro-organisms.

On the other hand, it seems to me that we are possibly disputing about the same thing, that what the one set of observers calls pus, the other set looks on as fibrinous exudation, for Klemperer, Ruijs, and others, speak of the occurrence of fibrinous exudation containing many leucocytes as the result of their injections. Certain it is that after the injection of these chemical substances, true creamy pus is not obtained unless

micro-organisms are present; the most that one gets is a
collection of putty-like material; and it becomes a question
whether this putty-like material may not simply be a further
change in what has been found at an early stage, and has then
presented the appearance of fibrinous exudation. Klemperer
states that, on examining a part into which croton oil has been
injected, the tissues at the centre of the irritation are of a
yellow colour, being infiltrated with fibrinous exudation and
large numbers of leucocytes. Where the pyogenic organisms
act, their peptonising action rapidly dissolves this original
tissue, and prevents the coagulation of the fresh exudation, and
thus a cavity containing fluid pus is produced. On the other
hand, where these organisms do not act, there are still grounds
for believing that the tissues themselves can, very slowly, it is
true, dissolve and remove the dead material, and thus we may
quite well find, as the result of the prolonged action of the
living cells on the extensive dead mass, a putty-like material
which has been described as pus.

This seems to me to be the most probable explanation of
these discrepant statements, but on this view we must admit
that these irritating substances cannot cause true acute suppuration when micro-organisms are absent; the result which
they produce is a different pathological process, corresponding
more closely with the formation of chronic abscesses than with
true acute suppuration. For the formation of acute abscesses
we apparently require the presence of the peptonising ferment
produced by the micro-organisms, or at any rate, of a chemical
substance which prevents coagulation of the exuded fluid.
Thus we have to note that both Grawitz and Scheuerlen, the
latter of whom denies the occurrence of suppuration as the
result of the application of irritating chemical substances, state
that they have succeeded in setting up abscesses by the injection of cadaverine, an alkaloid separated by Brieger from putrefying flesh; this substance is not only an irritant, but also
prevents coagulation.

I mention this experiment, but I am not quite satisfied as to its accuracy, and
should like to see it repeated carefully before I would lay great stress on it.—In

acute abscess formation we not only have the effused liquor sanguinis remaining fluid, but also solution of the original or of the inflammatory tissue. For this we require a chemical (peptonising) ferment, and the micro-organisms probably act in that they are constantly producing ammonia and other products, which keep up the irritation of the tissues and cause effusion of leucocytes and plasma, and also a chemical ferment which causes solution of the tissue much more rapidly than could occur as the result of the action of the tissues themselves. Ruijs, in the experiments previously alluded to, where he injected turpentine, etc., into the interior chamber of the eye, describes the result as follows :—At first the iris became hyperæmic and rapidly covered with a white exudation, which increased from day to day for about a week, and sometimes showed a few yellow points. This was clearly a fibrinous exudation adherent to, and infiltrating the iris. During the second week it became more yellowish in colour, and was gradually absorbed. On examination of this material it was found to consist of fibrin and leucocytes, and the iris and cornea were infiltrated with round cells, but there was no destruction of tissue. Where cocci were introduced, true suppuration with destruction of tissue occurred.

As a matter of fact, the only situations where we have to consider the possible occurrence of suppuration without micro-organisms are the surfaces of wounds and the skin and mucous membrane. With regard to the possibility of acute suppuration from the irritation of antiseptics applied to wounds, I must confess that I have never yet seen true creamy pus coming from the surface of a wound without finding micro-organisms in it; and I suspect that the antiseptic can only increase the amount of exudation and the number of leucocytes, and thus cause at most a semi-purulent discharge. At the margin of the alembroth dressings, pustules are apt to form on the skin, especially where the discharge is free, and these pustules contain a small quantity of sticky semi-purulent fluid, but no micro-organisms. This is the nearest approach that I have seen to acute suppuration in man without the action of micro-organisms.

It must be noted also with regard to these cases, that the process is quite superficial and leaves no scar ; there is no marked destruction of tissue.

LECTURE II.

THE PYOGENIC COCCI MAY BE PRESENT IN THE HUMAN BODY WITHOUT
CAUSING SUPPURATION OR SEPTIC DISEASES—*CONDITIONS NECESSARY FOR
INFECTION*—EMBOLISM—GENERAL AND LOCAL DEPRESSION OF VITALITY—
INFLAMMATION—COLD—INJURY—IRRITATING CHEMICAL SUBSTANCES—
THE SEAT OF INOCULATION AND THE ANATOMICAL ARRANGEMENT OF THE
PART.

In the last Lecture we saw that these pyogenic cocci are
constantly present in suppurative affections, that they can cause
suppuration both in animals and in man, as evidenced by experiments and also by the microscopical observation of the changes
which occur at the seat of infection, and that true acute suppuration does not occur naturally when these organisms are
absent. It would therefore appear as if with the discovery of
the pyogenic organisms, the etiology of acute suppurative affections was satisfactorily settled. This, however, is hardly the
case, for the following considerations among others render it
evident that, in most cases, other factors in addition to the micro-
organisms, must come into play.

Other Factors usually necessary.—Thus we find a great
variety of morbid processes caused by the same organisms.
The staphylococcus pyogenes aureus can set up a superficial
inflammation of the skin, a boil, an abscess, acute ulcerative
endocarditis, or even pyæmia; and the streptococcus pyogenes
causes sometimes phlegmonous inflammation, sometimes peritonitis, sometimes puerperal fever, and sometimes pyæmia.
Then, again, we have the fact on which I have not as yet
dwelt, that, in order to produce these suppurative affections in

animals, various conditions, such as the injection of large numbers of the micro-organisms are essential.

That these organisms are not of themselves able in most cases to set up suppurative diseases is evident also from the fact that they are frequently present in the blood without producing any suppurative affections. Thus Ogston states that in cases of septicæmia in man, the micrococci are present in the blood, and are excreted in a living state in the urine, and that without giving rise to secondary abscesses. Ogston's statement as to the presence of cocci in the blood has been confirmed by Von Eiselsberg, who examined the blood of almost all the cases in Billroth's clinique which were suffering from septic fever, and was able to demonstrate the presence of staphylococci and streptococci, most frequently of staphylococcus pyogenes albus, in the blood, and yet apparently no abscesses formed. In the case of acute osteo-myelitis also, Garré has found the pyogenic staphylococci in the blood, although the patients did not suffer from abscesses in more than one situation. In connection with acute osteo-myelitis, perhaps the most interesting observations, as showing that these organisms may exist in the blood without doing any harm, are those in which children have been born suffering from this disease, while the mothers, through whose blood only the organisms could have come, have apparently been in good health. As an example of this, I may mention the following case published by Rosenbach in a paper on acute osteo-myelitis.

E. A., aged thirty, was delivered of her fifth child in June 1858. She had been married ten years, and all her other children were living and healthy when born; she was not aware of having suffered any fright or injury to account for the disease in the child's leg. The latter, a full-grown boy, was born dead at full time, and had apparently been alive quite recently. Attention was at once drawn to the right leg, which was swollen, and showed distinct fluctuation both in front and behind. Immediately below the patella there was a bulla on the skin, the whole leg had a marked erysipelatous character, and on making an incision, a large quantity of pus was evacuated, and it was found that the greater portion of the soft parts of the leg was destroyed, and that there was scarcely any muscular substance to be seen. Further investigation showed that almost the whole of the periosteum of the tibia was detached, and the bone was in a state of necrosis. At the lower part, a small portion of the periosteum was inflamed, but still adherent to the bone; at the upper part the epiphysis of the tibia was almost entirely separated from the shaft, and was only connected with it by a few membranous threads.

Then we have a very interesting paper by Escherich on the presence of pyogenic cocci in the milk of women suffering from puerperal fever. In a considerable number of these cases he demonstrated the presence of the same pyogenic cocci in the milk from both breasts, and there was every reason to believe that the organisms had reached the milk from the blood, more especially there was an entire absence of any disease or ulceration of the nipple ; and yet, in these cases, there were apparently no abscesses either in the mamma or elsewhere. Escherich's observations have been confirmed by Longard, and both of these investigators have made experiments on animals, which had just brought forth young, which show that very shortly after the injection of these organisms into the blood they appear in the milk.

Escherich examined the milk in nine healthy women without finding micro-organisms in it, and he likewise failed to find them in five cases where the fever was due to other causes than puerperal fever, such as phthisis, syphilis, etc. Of thirteen cases of general septic infection, one gave a negative result, in one bacilli were present, in one cocci were found only in the milk from one breast, and in ten the same organisms were present in the milk from both breasts ; in none of these was there any excoriation of the nipple nor abscess in the glands. The prevailing organism was, in his opinion, staphylococcus albus (though their identity is denied by Longard), and in four cases aureus was found as well. Escherich believes that in these cases the organisms come from the uterine wound, pass into the blood, and are excreted with the milk.

These pyogenic cocci have also been found in the blood in various febrile diseases, and not necessarily in association with suppuration. Thus Loeffler found the streptococcus pyogenes, or an organism very closely resembling it, in the diphtheritic membrane in cases of scarlatinal sore throat, and he observed that in some cases these organisms penetrated from the surface into the body. Fraenkel and Freudenberg have also investigated the organisms of scarlet fever, and have found that the streptococcus pyogenes is present in the blood in a considerable number of cases, without, however, apparently giving rise to any suppurative or septic affections.

I need not go into further details to show that these micro-organisms do not necessarily of themselves set up suppuration and septic diseases when present in the body ; in the following considerations, sufficient evidence of this will be brought forward.

Conditions necessary for Infection.—The conditions which are necessary to enable these organisms to live and act in the body may be considered according as they chiefly affect the body, or according as they chiefly affect the microbe. We have also some conditions such as temperature, season of the year, locality, moisture, &c., which must be grouped under a third heading ; for, with regard to these, we do not know whether their influence is due to some action which they exert on the body, or to some effect which they produce on the microbe. In considering these conditions, it is not possible to draw a sharp line between the various groups, because a number of these conditions is almost always combined in the same case ; but I shall, as far as I can, endeavour to avoid repetition, and at the same time to treat of the various facts under their chief headings.

Had time permitted I should have liked, before entering on consideration of these conditions, to have traced the fate of the pyogenic organisms in the body when they fail to get the upper hand. And we should have found that these organisms disappear in a very remarkable manner from the blood, that they are in fact apparently rapidly killed in the blood, or deposited from it in various tissues and organs, or possibly excreted through the various excretory glands. The rapidity with which some organisms disappear from the blood is very remarkable ; it is, in many cases, a matter merely of minutes, certainly of an hour or two, and this disappearance of the organisms from the blood must be due to an active destructive action of the con-stituents of the blood on them ; mere unsuitability of soil is not sufficient to account for the rapidity of the phenomenon.

That organisms are very rapidly killed in the blood was shown long ago by Traube and Gscheidlen, and in a paper published in the *Pathological Transactions* in 1879, I referred to experiments which I had made, in which I found that twenty-four hours after intravenous injection of bacteria into rabbits, the organisms had disappeared completely from the blood. Von Fodor investigated this matter more precisely, injecting fluids containing known species of non-pathogenic organisms such as bac. subtilis, &c., into the jugular vein, and making cultivations from the blood at intervals, varying from four hours to several days ; and he found that where the animals were healthy, the organisms had markedly diminished in number in four hours, and had completely disappeared after some days. Wyssokowitsch has gone into this matter very fully in a paper which is full of precise and interesting details. He found that the rapidity with which micro-organisms disappeared from the blood varied with the species employed, and also with the condition of the microbe, more especially whether or not it was spore-bearing. Thus, when moderate quantities of *spirillum tyrogenum*, a non-pathogenic and non-spore-bearing organism, were injected into the blood stream, they were found in greatly diminished numbers after five minutes, and had completely disappeared in seven minutes. In the case of other similar organisms, their disappearance was complete in less than four hours. Spores were rapidly deposited in the blood, but retained their vitality for several days ; in the case of bacillus subtilis, a few were found alive even after seventy-eight days. They are apparently deposited in the endothelial cells of the small blood vessels, chiefly in the spleen. As regards the pyogenic organisms, the streptococcus pyogenes, which does not exert a pathogenic action when introduced into the veins of rabbits in small numbers, disappeared in forty hours, and was much reduced in number after seven hours : staphylococcus pyogenes aureus was still found in very small numbers after seven days, but their numbers had much diminished even after five and a quarter hours. From Wyssokowitsch's researches it is clear that, while part of the organisms die in the blood, part are deposited like particles of pigment in various organs ; and this is not only the case with non-pathogenic organisms, but seems also to take place with pathogenic ones. Thus, anthrax bacilli injected in comparatively small quantities into rabbits, were found to have disappeared from the blood after twenty-four hours, but were present in large numbers in the spleen and liver. Where larger quantities were introduced they were still present in the blood after that time, and in any case they reappeared in large numbers at a later period.

We should also have seen that there is good reason for believing that these organisms may be excreted by the various excretory glands, although this is a matter about which there is still considerable dispute. That they are so excreted by the kidneys is shown by various observations ; and this is an important point to remember, as probably explaining certain cases of pyelitis and bacteruria occurring in patients who have never had any instrument passed, and whose ureters and bladders are perfectly normal ; the occurrence of these cases being explained on the supposition that the organisms had entered the blood in a living state, were excreted by the kidneys, and afterwards, as in the example of which I showed a drawing at last lecture (see Fig. 4) (see paper on " Micrococci in relation to Wounds, &c.," *British Medical Journal,* July 1884) found a suitable pabulum in the urine, and grew in the pelvis of the kidney.

Wyssokowitsch and others deny the excretion of bacteria by the kidneys, and hold that they only appear in the urine after rupture of blood vessels, say in the glomeruli, and the passage of their contents into the tubules. That this may be the usual sequence of events I do not deny, but I still think that bacteria may be excreted by the kidneys in some cases. Ogston states that he has found micro-cocci in the urine of patients suffering from septicæmia, although apparently these patients had no disease of the kidney or bladder. Again, in pyæmia and various other diseases, for example in Ribbert's experiments with aspergillus, there is a marked tendency for the organisms to become located in the kidney, and this seems to me to point to some functional activity attracting and retaining the organisms. Ribbert found in his experiments on the fate of the cocci of osteo-myelitis in the blood, that after twenty-four hours the cocci could be demonstrated in all the organs by Gram's method, chiefly in the liver, but that they subsequently disappeared from all the organs except the kidney. He also found in animals killed after six hours, that there were large numbers of cocci in the convoluted and straight urinary tubules. Ribbert also states that a bacillus which he investi-gated in this respect was excreted by the kidney, but did not grow in the urinary tubules. Philipowicz states that anthrax bacilli, and also glanders and tubercle bacilli, appear in considerable numbers in the urine of mice and guinea-pigs, even where there is no lesion of the vessels.

As regards excretion from the mamma, I have referred to the observations and experiments made by Escherich and Longard; and these facts are of interest in connection with mammary abscess, as showing that the organisms which set up these abscesses may arrive at the gland from the blood, and either grow in the tissues or in the acini of the gland after excretion; although, without doubt, the great majority of abscesses of the mamma are caused by the spread of the organisms inwards, either along the milk ducts, or from cracks in the nipple.

Longard injected small quantities of cultivations of staphylococcus pyogenes aureus into the jugular veins of guinea-pigs, which had just been delivered of young. In one case he examined the milk, taken with suitable precautions, after four hours, and although he found a few cocci on microscopical examination, he was unable to demonstrate them by cultivation : they were, however, found after twenty-four hours. In another experiment Longard injected the organisms under the skin of a bitch, and here also they were present in the milk twenty-four hours later. In neither case was there any microscopical change in the mammæ. Escherich injected a mixture of albus and aureus into the left jugular vein, and he found that milk taken four hours later contained a pure cultivation of the white coccus. This animal had a retro-mammary abscess fourteen days later. In another experiment Escherich injected a large quantity of a similar mixture of organisms into the jugular vein of a bitch, and found cocci in the milk after three hours. When the animal died eight days later, capillary emboli of cocci were found in the mamma, and the cocci were also present in the tissue around the vessels. The rapid appearance of the cocci in the milk in these cases, and the absence of any apparent disease of the mamma, seems to me only explicable on the view that they were excreted by the gland.

We should also have seen reason to believe that the salivary glands, more especially the parotid, occasionally take part in this excretion of pyogenic organisms; thus again offering a possible explanation of the not infrequent occurrence of abscesses in the parotid gland after suppuration elsewhere.

It is, however, only right to say that some writers, Leyden for example, think that in these cases the cocci may have spread from the mouth along the salivary ducts, but this seems to me very unlikely. Hanau, however (reference in *Centralb. f. Bakteriologie*, vol. vi., No. 5) investigated five cases of secondary suppuration in the parotid, in which he concluded, from their position, that the organisms had spread into the gland along the duct from the mouth.

On the other hand, in a case of pyæmia with abscess in the prostate, Hanau came to the conclusion, likewise from the position of the organisms, that the abscess was due to excretion of the cocci from the blood.

Passet also found that cocci were excreted through the conjunctiva in the case of mice, and Longard is said to have confirmed this observation.

The study also of the exact mode in which the body carries on the battle with the microbes, more especially the study of the investigations which have been set on foot as the result of Metschnikoff's experiments on phagocytosis, would have furnished us with much interesting and suggestive material for consideration. And we should have seen what an important part the leucocytes play in the destruction of micro-organisms, and in the limitation of inflammatory processes, although the evidence does not as yet seem to be sufficient to support Metschnikoff's idea that these cells act by taking up the organisms into their interior and there killing them.

Metschnikoff's first research, published in 1884, had reference to a parasite observed in Daphnis, the parasite belonging possibly to the class of yeast fungi. The asci containing the spores are apparently swallowed by the Daphnis, and, probably as the result of the action of the gastric juice, the spores become free, and being pointed in shape pierce the wall of the intestine, and reach the interior of the animal. When this has occurred, a battle begins between the parasites and the blood corpuscles, and every spore or portion of a spore which penetrates into the body cavity, is quickly surrounded by blood corpuscles. The spores thus surrounded, apparently undergo degeneration, they become thick, irregular in outline, light yellow or brown and granular. The blood corpuscles unite to form finely granular pale plasmodia, which exhibit amœboid movements, and contain the granular remains of the spores. When, however, too many spores reach the body cavity, or when for some other reason the spores remain uninjured, disease occurs, the spores germinate and are carried by the blood-stream over the whole body, and are deposited in those parts where the blood flows most slowly—for example, in the front part of the head and in the neighbourhood of the tail; in these situations masses of fungus cells are formed.—In another research, Metschnikoff has studied the relation of anthrax bacilli to frogs. After introducing these bacilli under the skin of frogs, he states that the bacilli penetrate into the tissues and that a mass of lymphoid cells collects around the bacilli, and ultimately eats them up. (According to Cornil, this process can be readily observed by placing a little of the lymph from a frog on a glass slide under the microscope, and adding some anthrax bacilli. The lymph cells take up the anthrax bacilli into their interior, and the bacilli become granular and disappear.) The immunity of frogs against anthrax bacilli is probably due in part to the fact that the anthrax bacilli are not in a vigorous state at the ordinary temperature of cold-blooded animals.— Metschnikoff has also extended his observations to erysipelas in man. He investigated seven cases of erysipelas, of which two died. In these two cases there were numerous cocci in the cutis and in the subcutaneous tissue, and the cocci were always free and not in cells. In those cases, on the other hand, which ended in recovery, the state of matters was quite different, the inflammatory infiltration was more marked, and the leucocytes frequently contained cocci, while others contained irregular granules and others again were empty. Only a few cocci were present between the cells, along with small leucocytes which he terms "microphagocytes." There were also larger cells, which he terms "macrophagocytes," but these did not contain any cocci, and apparently ate up the microphagocytes. In the case of anthrax, Metschnikoff looks on the larger cells as the destructive agents, the smaller cells apparently not taking part in the process. Metschnikoff holds that animals which are immune against a certain disease, are those whose leucocytes can eat up the parasites, and that those animals which are not immune are those whose leucocytes cannot do this. He, however, apparently admits that pure phagocytosis is not always the whole process, for he has shown that bacillus anthracis becomes attenuated in the blood of immune sheep without having become enclosed in cells, and he thinks that the cells may act not only by intracellular digestion, but also by secreting injurious materials. He has further drawn attention to the fact that fever temperatures may act injuriously on the bacteria (*Fortschr. d. Med.*, 1887).

Metschnikoff's views have been opposed by several observers, and Holmfeld points out that it is just in the case of the most virulent diseases, such as mouse septicæmia and tuberculosis, that there is a marked tendency for the cells to take up the parasites, while on the other hand, bacteria, which are comparatively little dangerous for the animals, such as the pyogenic cocci, are almost never taken up by the leucocytes. Holmfeld has studied the behaviour of anthrax bacilli in warm-blooded animals, for he does not think that Metschnikoff's experiments on frogs give a fair view of the state of matters. He has employed susceptible animals such as rabbits and mice, and also non-susceptible animals such as rats, and he has used both virulent and attenuated bacilli. In mice and rats, the place selected for inoculation was the root of the tail; in rabbits, the base of the ear. Great care was taken to purify the skin, and to prevent the entrance of other organisms. The part was examined after twenty-four hours, and usually twenty-four hours later. The following are in a few words the results of his experiments :

When the virulent organisms are injected sub-cutaneously into rabbits and mice, œdema results, the fluid being clear and serous, and containing numerous bacilli, but no or almost no pus corpuscles ; nor do the corpuscles increase in number during the next twenty-four hours, and suppuration does not occur. In rats, on the other hand, there is always pus in the wound, its quantity bearing a relation to the virulence of the material introduced, and to the susceptibility of the animal inoculated ; thus in young rats, which are more susceptible than old rats, there is a muddy sero-purulent fluid containing numerous anthrax bacilli and corpuscles, while the older the rat the more does the material approach pure pus. Subcutaneous injection of attenuated anthrax bacilli into rabbits caused, as Metschnikoff has also stated, a slight local inflammation accompanied by suppuration. At the seat of inoculation there is constantly a drop of thick pus. Holmfeld's observations led him to believe that the bacteria die as the result of a chemical biological action rather than by digestion in the interior of the cells. In insusceptible animals, the cells evidently play only a small part, for in the pus there are comparatively few bacteria in cells, the great majority are free in the fluid, and most of them are killed without ever having been taken up by the cells. The conditions were the same when virulent material was employed, in so far that a few cells also contained bacilli. In rats the bacilli die in the pus in two to three days. Holmfeld also took pus, after twenty-four hours, containing living anthrax bacilli, and kept it in capillary tubes at 37° C., and found that in a day or two the bacilli were dead, although the cells had not taken them up. He concludes that the organisms are killed by some chemical material in the pus.

Wyssokowitsch explained the disappearance of the organisms which he injected into the blood-stream, not as the result of a battle between the leucocytes and the bacteria, but as the result of a battle between the bacteria and the endothelial cells of the capillaries in which he found the organisms deposited. The result of this battle is either that the bacteria die and disappear, or that the cells are killed by the bacteria, and thus furnish a nutritive substratum for their growth. With regard to these views Baumgarten, who also fails to be convinced of the truth of Metschnikoff's theory, points out that on Wyssokowitsch's own admission, only part of the bacteria were present in the cells, that others were free and adhered to the inner wall of the capillaries, and that probably, from the analogy with pigment granules, not a few were free in the parenchyma of the organs. Hence he cannot agree that the majority are killed within cells, and if this is not the case, then the question arises whether their inclusion in the cells has any significance at all in regard to the death of the organisms. He thinks that many species of bacteria die in the body simply because the peculiar constitution of the living material is unsuitable for their growth and development. It seems to me, however, that bacteria die too rapidly to allow of this explanation, for they do not die so quickly when their nutriment is exhausted outside the body.

Ribbert, in studying the death of fungi in the body, found that in the liver the sprouting spores of aspergillus were very quickly surrounded on all sides by a layer of leucocytes, while in the kidneys, muscles, &c., the inflammatory cell formation occurs relatively later. He explains the fact that in the liver, in this disease, the deposits of fungi are never so much developed as they are in the kidney, muscles, &c., by supposing that, in the liver, the early formation of this wall of leucocytes prevents the access of nutrient material and of oxygen to the growing mycelium, thus to a certain extent starving and choking them. Baumgarten does not agree with this explanation, for he cannot understand how, if this is the case, a similar effect is not produced on the microbes of pyæmia, tuberculosis, glanders, &c., and he thinks that if cells act at all, it is more likely that the fixed tissue cells are the active agents than the leucocytes.

The idea that disease is a battle between the tissue cells and the parasites was long ago upheld by Virchow, and in my book on antiseptic surgery I pointed out the great influence exerted by healthy tissues and blood clot in preventing the development of micro-organisms in wounds. It seems to stand to reason that something of this kind must occur, but whether Metschnikoff is correct in supposing that the digestive action of the cells is the important factor is quite another matter. When two forms of saprophytic bacteria are growing together, and one gets the upper hand, it does not do so by feeding on the others, but either by abstracting their nutriment or by forming products which are either directly poisonous to them or at any rate render the soil unsuitable for their growth. In the case of the body it may be that the organisms are killed by chemical substances given off by the leucocytes or the tissues, and not by inclusion and digestion in the cells. That they do disappear in the presence of leucocytes is evident from the facts which I have mentioned with regard to the relation of micrococci to the walls of abscesses.

I must, however, omit the consideration of these matters and pass on to the discussion of the conditions which enable or hinder these organisms to act; and the first condition, and an essential one, which we have to notice is, that an opportunity must be afforded to the organisms of resting for a time in the part in which they exert their action. If they are floating in the blood-current, they must be arrested at some part, and not only must they be arrested, but as we shall see, they must find at that spot conditions suitable for their growth.

EMBOLISM.

Such mechanical conditions causing the arrest of organisms are brought about by embolism, thrombosis, injury, &c. The importance of arrest of organisms has been beautifully shown by Ribbert in some experiments which he performed with a pathogenic species of mucor. When the spores of pathogenic aspergilli are injected into the blood, deposits are formed in various organs and also in large numbers in the various muscles. In the case of mucor, however, Ribbert noticed that while the spores when injected into the blood-stream gave rise to deposits in various organs, the muscles remained only slightly or not at all affected. On looking into the matter, it was seen that the spores of mucor were very small, much smaller than those of aspergillus, and Ribbert thought it possible that the reason why masses occurred in the muscles in the latter case and not in the former, was that on account of the larger size of the aspergillus spores they were caught in the capillaries of the muscles while the mucor spores passed through them. He therefore sought to increase the size of the mucor spores before their injection into the blood, and this he did by keeping them for a short time in a nutrient fluid at the temperature of the body. As a consequence, the spores swelled up and commenced to sprout, and when he found, under the microscope, that this had occurred, he injected the material into the circulation. The result corresponded entirely to his expectations, in contrast to the control experiments he found that in these cases fairly numerous deposits of fungi were present, not only in the organs but also in the muscles of the back and extremities.

Referring, however, more especially to experiments with the pyogenic organisms, we have several facts of a similar nature with regard to their action on rabbits. The injection of moderate quantities of staphylococcus pyogenes aureus into the circulation of rabbits is followed, as a rule, only by abscesses in the kidneys, the other organs apparently remaining unaffected ; but a number of experiments which have been made, among others by Ribbert, on the production of myocarditis and endocarditis in these animals, have shown that abscesses can be set up in other organs if the pyogenic cocci are attached to gross particles which cannot pass the capillaries of these organs. Thus Ribbert was able to produce myocarditis by using a cultivation of staphylococcus pyogenes aureus on potatoes, if he took care in removing the cultivation from the surface of the potato, to scrape off also the superficial layer of the potato itself. If this mixture of potato granules and organisms was rubbed up with water, so as to form a fine emulsion, and then injected into the circulation, the result was the production of deposits of organisms in the muscular tissue of the heart, as well as in other organs, leading to myocarditis ; if the particles of potato were very fine, only myocarditis resulted, but if they were coarser, endocarditis occurred as well.

Bonomé investigated nine cases of gangrene of the lungs in man, and found in three of them staphylococcus pyogenes aureus alone, in five staphylococcus pyogenes albus alone, and in one both organisms together. He tried to set up gangrene of the lungs in rabbits by the injection of these organisms into the circulation, but he failed to do so if only cultivations were employed. He succeeded, however, by taking pieces of the pith of the elder tree, breaking them up into very fine fragments, mixing these fragments with the cultivations of the pyogenic organisms, and then injecting this mixture into the jugular vein; the result was the formation of numerous deposits of cocci in the lungs leading, as shown last day, to extensive coagulation necrosis of large tracts of these organs, and, as a consequence, to extensive gangrene of the lungs. Injection of the fragments of the pith alone caused no effect.

In the same way, Ruijs found that if he injected a small quantity of a fluid cultivation of staphylococcus pyogenes aureus into the uninjured eyes of rabbits, suppuration did not result, and he concluded that the reason was that the cocci were carried away too quickly by the lymph stream; for if he soaked sterilised cotton threads in the cultivations, and then introduced portions of these threads into the anterior chamber of the eye, suppurative pan-ophthalmitis occurred.

The last experiment that I shall mention is one by Pawlowsky, who found that by the simultaneous injection of sterilised cinnobar and of cultivations of staphylococcus pyogenes aureus into the circulation, he produced abscesses in various organs, in fact the typical picture of pyæmia.

Etiology of Pyæmia.—The great importance of these facts, in explanation of the etiology of pyæmia, will be at once evident. Whether cases of pyæmia occur in man, like those described by Koch in the case of rabbits, as the result of the growth of cocci in the blood, their entanglement of blood corpuscles, and the consequent formation of emboli, we do not know; but it is very doubtful if this takes place, for the same cocci which seem to be the cause of pyæmia may, as we have said before, be often present in the blood in considerable numbers, without causing abscess

or embolism.   It is easy, however, to understand that the
ordinary pyogenic cocci may cause pyæmia, if they enter the
blood attached to portions of blood clot or other solid material.
This, in fact, is evident from the experiments mentioned, and
thus the importance of thrombosis and embolism, as factors in
the production of pyæmia, is clearly established.   These emboli
are not always necessarily emboli composed of detached portions
of blood clot ; in some cases probably, especially where the
streptococcus pyogenes is the active agent, the organisms grow
in the lymphatic vessels and the emboli are formed there, and
arrive at the blood with the lymph stream.   Probably in
pyæmia other factors also come into play, such as a large dose
of the organisms, general depression of vitality, possibly also
greater virulence of the organisms ; but it is evident from these
considerations, and from the clinical and pathological facts, that
embolism must play an important part.   Pyæmia must thus be
clearly distinguished from multiple abscesses, the so-called
chronic pyæmia, where embolism does not probably play any
part, but where cocci are able to circulate in the blood, and are
deposited in some part weakened by injury or other depressing
cause.

Arrest of Organisms not usually Sufficient.—The mere arrest
of these pyogenic organisms in the circulation, although an
important factor, is not, however, as a rule, sufficient of itself to
lead to the production of disease.   This is very well seen in the
case of rabbits.   Inject a considerable number of pyogenic
cocci into the circulation of a rabbit, and kill it within twenty-
four hours, it will be found that masses of organisms are present
in the capillaries of the lungs, and other organs of the body ;
but allow such an animal to live for forty-eight or seventy-two
hours, and it will be seen on killing it, that the organisms have
disappeared from the various organs, with the exception of the
kidneys (Ribbert).   Here we have evidence that although the
organisms had been able to stick in the various organs, the
other conditions were not favourable for their growth and
action ; and in the case of embolism, it is probable that the

material to which the cocci are attached of itself aids their growth, by causing injury to the endothelium of the blood-vessels, and thus leading to the production of a weak spot. And in the case of emboli composed of blood clot, the emboli are saturated with the products of the cocci, and are thus still more likely to injure the part. We must, therefore, pass on to the consideration of other conditions which aid the action of these organisms, and the chief of these is what we may roughly term general and local depression of vitality.

GENERAL DEPRESSION OF VITALITY.

That general depression of vitality can enable these organisms to live in the blood for a considerable time has been shown by a number of experiments. For example: I found in experiments on the presence or absence of organisms in the living tissues, that while organisms were absent when the animal was in a good state of health, yet if the vitality of the animal was depressed—say by administering large doses of phosphorus for some time—organisms could be found at times in the blood and tissues of the body. The same conclusion must be drawn from the following experiment:—If, of a putrefying fluid not containing pathogenic organisms, varying quantities are injected into the circulation of animals, it will generally be found that after twenty-four hours the organisms have died out in those animals which received a small dose; while in those in which a larger quantity—say 1 ccm.—was injected, in other words, in those whose vitality was depressed by the introduction at the same time of a quantity of the poisonous chemical products of these bacteria, organisms may still be found alive. This is a fact which has been confirmed by a number of observers, but as I shall have again to refer to experiments from which similar conclusions may be drawn, I shall pass on to what is much more important for the matter under discussion, viz., the result of local depression of vitality.

Wyssokowitsch has arrived at the same result in the research referred to in the note on p. 34, and Von Fodor also found a difference in the rapidity with which organisms were destroyed in the blood according as the animals were healthy or otherwise.

The following striking experiment on frogs with the bacilli of Rauschbrand, shows very well the effect of general depression of vitality, and how the virus may remain in the body without producing any effect till the vitality is diminished. Arloing, Cornevin, and Thomas placed frogs, some of which were inoculated with Rauschbrand and others not, in vessels containing water at 22° C. After fifteen to thirty hours the inoculated frogs died, and in the contents of the lymph sac the Rauschbrand bacilli were present in such numbers and of such virulence that their inoculation on warm-blood animals produced the ordinary results. The inoculated frogs remained well. In contrast with this, frogs inoculated with Rauschbrand, and kept in cold water, were unaffected.

LOCAL DEPRESSION OF VITALITY.

A number of experiments show that when the vitality of a part has been lowered by cutting off the blood-current for a comparatively short time, organisms grow in that part much more readily and luxuriantly than if the blood-stream had not been interfered with. To mention one or two examples:— According to Cornil, a septic nephritis is readily obtained by ligaturing the renal arteries for some hours, and then after removal of the ligature, injecting pyogenic organisms into the blood.

Bonomé found that direct injection of staphylococci into the kidneys was followed by necrosis, and later by suppuration along the track of the needle, but this was more extensive and followed more quickly if the renal arteries had previously been temporarily ligatured for two hours.

Heubner's experiments on the artificial production of diphtheria also show in a very marked manner the effect of local depression of vitality as the result of cutting off the blood-stream temporarily. Heubner arrested the circulation in the fundus of the bladder for two hours by the application of a ligature to the vesical arteries; after removal of the ligature there resulted intense congestion and œdema of the sub-mucous tissue, while, at the same time, as a consequence of the temporary inanition, the epithelial cells died; after the circulation was again restored there was a great exudation of blood plasma and cells, in fact, coagulation necrosis occurred on the mucous surface. Heubner found that if at the same time that the circulation was restored, septic bacteria were injected into the blood, they accumulated in large numbers in the affected part of the mucous membrane of the bladder, and set up extensive disease. In order to obtain these results, it is, however, necessary that large numbers of bacteria should be present in the blood, and this factor can only very rarely come into play in nature where the number of bacteria which enter the body at one time is seldom sufficiently great. Thus in the case of strangulated hernia, even where the circulation has been arrested for a considerable time, comparatively little harm is done, and unless actual gangrene of the bowel wall has occurred, bacteria are very seldom found in the fluid contained in the sac of the hernia, nor does suppurative peritonitis occur, for the number of pyogenic cocci in the intestinal canal is very small.—In conclusion, I may mention an experiment by Cornil, who states that if a slight nephritis is set up, either by cantharides or in some other way, and if then pyogenic organisms are injected into the blood, a septic peritonitis occurs. This last experiment leads us to the consideration of a very important factor in the production of local depression of vitality, viz., inflammation.

Inflammation.—Inflammation is frequently looked on as a predisposing cause of these suppurative diseases, and it has been held that inflammation leads to the formation of a weak spot where bacteria can settle and develope, and that while inflammation can be set up by other causes than micro-organisms, the pyogenic cocci are very apt to become added to it, and then suppuration results. On the other hand, in old times when wounds were allowed to become septic, it was generally held that the patient was safer when the surface of the wound had become covered with granulations, than before granulation had taken place. We have also seen, in considering the anatomy of abscess, that as the granulation tissue increased in amount, so the penetration of the organisms into the body was rendered difficult, and they remained more and more limited to the interior of the abscess. In the case of erysipelas the cessation of the inflammation seems to stand in some relation to the accumulation of leucocytes in the part. In the case of tubercles also, which consist of a central mass of epithelioid

cells and an outer wall of leucocytes, I believe that the external
circle is purely an inflammatory circle, and is of great importance
in limiting the spread of the tubercle bacilli. That, however,
preliminary inflammation is not essential to enable the pyogenic
organisms to act, is shown by many facts, such as Garré's and
Bockhardt's experiments on themselves, and by similar experiments performed by Grawitz with reference to acne contagiosa
of horses where the organisms which are the cause of the
disease produce it when merely rubbed into the skin.

To explain the facts of the case, I must shortly recall the
chief points as regards inflammation. Inflammation which has
gone on for some time may be divided into three stages. In the
first stage we have the preliminary dilatation (or it may be in
some rare cases, contraction) of the vessels, the increased flow
of blood through the part, and, along with this, increased flow
of lymph, soon followed by slowing of the circulation, and ultimately by inflammatory stasis with, at the same time, exudation
of blood plasma and corpuscles. In the second stage, the
irritation is continued, and the tissue originally attacked by the
inflammation is removed and its place taken by granulation
tissue. In the third stage, the irritation has ceased, and retro-
gressive changes occur, leading to the formation of a scar.

If we consider the state of the tissues in these three stages,
we see that in the first stage, as was long ago pointed out by
Sir Joseph Lister, the vital activity of the tissue is suspended,
the functions of the part are, so to speak, paralysed, in other
words, the tissue has become an extremely weak tissue, and one
unable to resist in any way the entrance of the parasites. In
the second stage, this weak tissue has been removed, and its
place has been taken by young, vigorous, healthy, granulation
tissue, which has probably great power in repelling the attacks
of the organisms. Lastly, in the third stage, this granulation
tissue is getting older and becoming converted into less active
tissue. The first stage of inflammation is partly defensive and
partly reparative, and always occurs after every injury. The
second stage may be looked on as a purely defensive stage, the
irritant still continuing to act. In the third stage, the irritant

has gone, and processes leading to permanent repair take place.

The relation of inflammation to infection may perhaps be best illustrated by regarding it as an instance of instinctive action. The first effect of the irritant is to damage the part, and the first result is dilatation of the blood-vessels and increased flow of blood and lymph; the part in fact is flushed with blood as if an attempt were being made to wash away the irritating cause (Landerer). This is a process which is probably constantly occurring in our bodies with satisfactory results. If the irritant continues to act it is very soon found that these attempts are ineffectual, and the next instinctive method of protection is to get rid of the injured tissues and to supply their place by young, strong, healthy tissue, granulation tissue. Finally, when the irritating cause has been got rid of, the vigilance of the part is, so to speak, relaxed, and the tissues proceed to develope into a less active and less vigorous tissue, viz., fibrous tissue.

The uses of inflammation are not always apparent; the process is not guided by reason. The natural instinct of the tissues is, so to speak, to resent intrusion, and their mode of showing resentment is by inflammation. In some cases, as in erysipelas, this inflammation may be too late to be of any use in repelling the intruder, which has already passed on before the inflammatory changes have had time to occur. In other cases, the inflammation may be immoderate in amount and lead to extensive destructive changes—more extensive than those caused by the infective agent. Or again, the inflammation may weaken the tissues, and in the case of some organisms, the very attempt to resist their entrance may just open up the way for their action.

Clinically, the organisms enter during the first and last stages, more especially during the first, and not, as a rule, during the intermediate stage, unless, indeed, while growing outside the new tissue, on the surface of the wound, they can so injure it as to reduce it again to the position of a weak tissue—to the first stage in fact. This is very well shown in a series of experiments made by Huber on the localisation of virus. Huber performed his experiments on rabbits, and set up inflammation in one ear by rubbing in croton oil, the other ear being left intact for purposes of control. The infective material employed was virulent anthrax bacilli, and these were introduced into the body as far as possible from the seat of inflammation, viz., at the root of the tail. According to the stage of inflammation which he desired to study, Huber applied the croton oil before or after the infection with anthrax bacilli. The result of these experiments was in the first place that the bacilli were not found outside the vessels in the tissues of the inflamed part in any stage of the inflammation; and in the second place, that their presence inside the vessels was dependent on the stage of the local affection. Thus, in the first stage, where there was inflammatory œdema—this stage reaching its height in about seven and a half hours—there was a very marked increase in the number of the bacilli in the capillaries of the inflamed part, as compared with the number which were present in a similar part of the opposite ear. As the inflammation passed into the second stage, the number of bacilli in the capillaries of the inflamed part gradually diminished, till when this stage was at its height—after forty-eight hours—the bacilli had completely disappeared, although they were present in large numbers in the capillaries of the other ear. During the third stage, where the inflammation had subsided, and where new tissue was being formed, bacilli again appeared, and were found in considerable numbers in the newly-formed vessels. Ultimately, when the scar had been formed, there was no difference as regards the number of bacilli in the capillaries of the scar, and the number in the capillaries elsewhere.

It has been found as regards the pyogenic cocci, that if they are circulating in the blood, the induction of a severe inflammatory action does not lead to their deposit in the part, while if the inflammation is less severe, they can apparently pass out of the blood-vessels, and set up suppuration. Thus Rinne concludes from his experiments on suppuration that a violent inflammatory action did not produce a *locus minoris resistentiæ*, but that the slighter injury caused by the chemical products of the bacteria sufficiently weakened the part to enable the organisms to grow in it. Acute osteo-myelitis and local tubercular diseases frequently stand in some relation to injury, but they are not, as a rule, attributed to severe injuries, but usually to some slight blow or sprain. In a phthisical individual, fracture of a bone or some other severe injury, is not followed by the development of a local tuberculosis, whereas a slight sprain is very commonly mentioned as the exciting cause of such a process, the probability being that the severe injury sets up too great reaction to permit the organisms to act, while the slighter injury simply weakens the part.

Cold.—Another point which has been much discussed in relation to inflammation and suppuration is the effect of cold. It is generally assumed that cold is a frequent cause, or at least a very predisposing cause of inflammation, as, for example, in the production of pneumonia. That cold may play an important part as one of the factors in that disease is very probable, but it is needless for me to say that we are constantly subjected to violent changes of temperature, without the production of inflammatory disease, so that it seems as if when a result is obtained, some other factor comes into play.

Fraenkel, in his papers on pneumonia, points out that, as the organisms held by him to be the causal agents are frequently present in the respiratory tracts of healthy individuals, other causes, among which he mentions cold, must play an important part.

That cold can cause inflammatory affections where the conditions are suitable, is evident as regards the external surface of the body, from the production of chilblains, the tissue thus weakened being brought into a condition rendering it very liable to attack from organisms. As regards the effects of cold on the internal parts of the body, some very interesting observations have been made by Lassar. A number of rabbits were shaved or deprived of their hair in some way or other; these animals when kept at a suitable and equable temperature (about 20° C.) and well fed, remained in good health, but on being taken out of the warm room and plunged into ice-cold water for from one to three minutes, then dried carefully, chafed and warmed again, they almost always in the course of one or two days showed albuminuria, increasing at a later period often

D

to a great extent, and accompanied by the presence of hyaline cylinders in the urine; at the same time the rectal temperature was as much as 1·5° C. above the normal. These animals often recovered from the albuminuria, but were again similarly affected when again exposed to cold. On microscopical examination of the organs, they were seen to be in what Lassar terms a state of "interstitial inflammation"; the organs chiefly affected being the kidneys and liver, but also in some cases the lungs, muscular tissue of the heart, and the sheaths of the nerves. In the organs it was seen that there was no degeneration of the interstitial tissues, but the blood-vessels, especially in the lungs and liver, were often enormously dilated, the arteries filled with thrombi, and large numbers of leucocytes were present in the tissues in the neighbourhood of the veins. The effect of cold in these experiments seems, in fact, to be the production of what is probably a weak tissue, and one therefore liable to attack from organisms.

As to the relation of pyogenic organisms to animals acted on by cold, I only know of experiments by Grawitz on the relation of peritonitis to cold, but his experiments are not sufficiently satisfactory. He shaved the skin of the abdomen in young animals, covered it for from a half to one hour with warm compresses, and then suddenly removing these, allowed a draught of ice-cold air to play on the part for twenty to forty minutes. This caused no bad effect on the peritoneum, nor was any bad result produced on that membrane when organisms were simultaneously injected into the intestinal canal or into the blood; and in one experiment the cocci were injected directly into the abdominal cavity, also without setting up peritonitis. In the last experiment, however, the cocci were injected three quarters of an hour before the commencement of the exposure to cold, and it is highly probable that, under the circumstances, they had died, or had been removed by the healthy peritoneum before the application of the cold; and this is the more likely to have been the case, seeing that the activity of the peritoneum was probably increased, as the result of the warm compresses applied to the skin over the abdomen.

Injury.—An important cause, predisposing to the occurrence of suppuration, is injury, which probably acts in two ways; in the first place, by setting up the early stage of inflammation; and in the second place, by leading to effusion of blood, and thus enabling any pyogenic cocci which may be circulating in the blood to pass out of the vessels, and find in the cellular tissue a suitable place for their development.

The effect of injury is well shown in experiments which have been made on the production of acute endocarditis. In order to induce this disease in animals, by injection of the pyogenic cocci into the blood, it has been found either that the number of cocci employed must be very large, or that they must be attached to gross particles, as has already been mentioned, or that some injury must be caused to the valves before their injection. Wyssokowitsch and others have performed experiments of this kind, and have found that by introducing a rod into the jugular vein, they were able to cause laceration of the valves, and that then, on subsequent injection of staphylococci into the blood, ulcerative endocarditis occurred. The effect of the injury in this instance is no doubt chiefly to lead to loss of resisting power in the endothelial and connective tissue cells, as the result of the early stage of inflammation induced by it.

The relation of injury to certain inflammatory diseases in man is generally accepted, and I need only instance the case of acute osteo-myelitis which is frequently attributed to an injury. In experiments on animals, with regard to the production of acute osteo-myelitis, it is, as a rule, necessary not only to inject the pyogenic organisms into the blood, but also to cause some injury to the bone. If this is done, especially where large numbers of cocci are introduced into the circulation, the animals generally die in from twelve to fourteen days, much emaciated, and showing pus at the seat of fracture, pus in the medulla and necrosis of bone. With regard to man, there are several cases on record in which the relation of injury to this disease is very strikingly shown; and the fact that the disease occurs much more often in males than females, and especially in young males, is usually attributed to the fact that injuries are sustained more frequently by boys than girls. At the same time, the number of cases of acute osteo-myelitis in man, in which the direct relation to an injury can be satisfactorily traced, is in reality comparatively small ; and that injury, though it plays a part in some instances, is not an essential condition for the production of the disease, is shown by its occurrence after acute fevers, and also by the fact that it is limited, as a rule, to certain favourite seats. When, however, the disease affects bones or parts of bones which are not usually attacked, a history of injury or exposure to cold can generally be obtained to explain its occurrence in these abnormal situations. In the case of wounds also, we must not forget that the injury done to the surface of a wound during an operation by the knife and the manipulations, sets up the early stage of inflammation, and that thus the surface of a wound is for a few hours at any rate a weak surface, and one unable to resist attacks from organisms.

That one great explanation of the value of injury in aiding the occurrence of suppurative diseases is the extravasation of blood from the vessels is shown in a very striking manner by experiments on symptomatic anthrax, a disease to which I shall have to allude in detail presently. I may say here that this disease is caused by bacilli, but is not set up if the bacilli are introduced into the circulating blood ; in order to produce it the bacilli must act in the cellular tissue. After injection of the organisms into the blood, the animals remain well, and the bacilli very soon disappear ; if, however, shortly after the injection of the bacilli into the blood, a bruise is produced in some part of the body, the bacilli pass out of the vessels into the cellular tissue along with the blood, grow there, and soon cause the formation of the characteristic tumours, the spread of the disease, and its fatal termination. In man it is sometimes seen that bruises in weakly individuals are followed by suppuration, and I have already published the case of a drunkard who had albuminuria, and was in a very low state of health, and who, whenever he received a bruise, developed an abscess at that part. In his depressed state, the pyogenic cocci were probably able to live in his blood, and the injuries, by setting up the early stage of inflammation, and thus further weakening the tissues, and also by leading to the effusion of blood containing the organisms, gave rise to the formation of abscesses.

Irritating Chemical Substances.—Another important cause of depression of vitality is the presence of irritating chemical substances. The mode of action of these chemical substances is probably that, when concentrated, they destroy the vitality of the tissue by their caustic effect, and when more dilute, they set up the early stage of inflammation, which also occurs in the former case in the vicinity of the dead part. The effect of these substances in procuring a weak spot at which the organisms can develop, is no doubt the explanation of Kocher's results with regard to acute osteo-myelitis in dogs. He found that if digestive disturbances were induced by the introduction of large quantities of septic material into the intestinal canal, and if, at the same time, a bone was injured by the injection of ammonia or other irritating chemical substances into it, acute osteo-myelitis occurred at the seat of injury, while the injection of the chemical substances alone only produced temporary reaction. These experiments, however, were only few in number, and are not completely satisfactory, because it is possible that the organisms spread in along the needle track, and did not reach the part from the blood. It has also been found that if irritating chemical substances are injected subcutaneously into rabbits, and if, at the same time, large numbers of pyogenic cocci are injected into the veins, suppuration frequently occurs at the seat of injection, the suppuration going hand in hand with the development of the pyogenic organisms which have reached the part from the blood (Biondi).

Many of the former experiments on the production of suppuration by means of irritating chemical substances, which frequently resulted in growth of micro-organisms in the part, and, as a consequence, the occurrence of suppuration, show how the presence of irritating chemical substances placed the parts in a condition which diminished their resisting power against the action of micro-organisms. Grawitz and de Bary found that if croton oil was injected into rabbits subcutaneously, it caused inflammation, and sometimes, in their opinion, suppuration ; if, however, the pyogenic organisms were also present, suppuration always occurred, although these cocci alone in small numbers are unable to produce suppuration in the normal subcutaneous tissue of dogs or rabbits.

If I may venture to apply these facts to the treatment of wounds, it seems to me that if the views which I have attempted to develop as to the importance of a granulation wall as a barrier against micro-organisms are correct, it is questionable whether, in the case of wounds which have become septic, it is well to wash them out with irritating antiseptics, as is so often done at present. That it is well to remove the decomposing discharge both by free drainage and also by washing out the wound in some cases is of course evident, but where strong irritating antiseptics are employed, unless they are able to kill all the micro-organisms present in the wound, and thus render it aseptic, the result of their injection might be, I think, that they will injure the granulation wall, and thus produce a weak spot in which the pyogenic cocci present in the wound can develop, and through which they may be enabled to enter the body. Thus it has been found that in cases of tubercular disease of bones and joints, accompanied by suppuration, general tuberculosis, more especially tubercular meningitis, occurs by far most frequently where the sinuses have become septic, and more especially where, in addition, these septic sinuses have been much irritated by futile antiseptic injections. Hence it seems to me that, except in cases where there is reasonable ground for believing that the injection of these antiseptics into septic wounds will completely eradicate the organisms, it is better to avoid the use of irritating antiseptics such as carbolic acid, and if it is thought well to wash away the discharge, to employ some fluid which will not injure the granulation wall.

Except in the case of wounds, the chemical substances which aid in enabling the bacteria to gain a foothold, are the products of the organisms themselves. That various bacterial products are highly poisonous is now well known, and in the case of putrefactive and pyogenic organisms these products are able not only to cause local trouble, but also to set up fever, to depress the vitality of the patient, or it may be even to cause death. With regard to these general effects of the chemical products of bacteria, it is unnecessary for me to enter into further detail, for the fact is now so well known that in most books on surgery we find, in addition to septicæmia and pyæmia, a third group of general septic diseases, due to the action of these products, described under the title of septic intoxication or, as Dr. Matthews Duncan has termed it, sapræmia. I may, therefore, at once pass on to the local effects of the products of bacteria and their action in enabling the organisms to live and multiply in the part.

I need only mention in this respect Panum's well-known researches, in which he found that although he destroyed the bacteria present in a putrefying liquid, he still had a fluid which, in sufficient quantities, was intensely poisonous and rapidly caused the death of the animal. The same was the case in Koch's experiments, in which he found that the injection of a large quantity of putrefying fluid into mice frequently occasioned the rapid death of the animal, while if a minute amount only was introduced, the animals either survived or fell victims to 'some infective disease, the result of the development of bacteria. A number of these poisonous bases, the products of putrefactive fermentation, have now been isolated by Brieger.

Products of the Bacteria themselves.—In some experiments which I performed recently with an organism described by Hauser under the name of *proteus vulgaris* — an organism not uncommonly present in putrefying materials—I diluted the growth in gelatine with a certain amount of water before injection. In some cases, however, I used for dilution, instead of water, boiled meat infusion, in which the same organisms had been growing, that is to say, a fluid containing the products of the growth of these bacteria, and I found, for example, that while one-fortieth c.c.m. of the mixture prepared by the addition of water never killed the animals experimented on, where the dilution was made to the same degree with the boiled meat infusion, the animals died from the same dose after about forty-eight hours. In the second case, a larger quantity of the products of the bacteria—these products being very poisonous—was introduced than in the first case, and to this we must ascribe the difference in the result. In experiments on guinea pigs with the cholera bacillus, Hueppe has found that infection occurs more certainly and with less material, if there has been preliminary action on the intestine of the poisonous products of the cholera bacilli, or even of the ptomaines of other bacteria; and Flügge and Wyssokowitsch have shown that bacteria which are not usually pathogenic in the animals employed for the experiments, can penetrate into tissues previously weakened by bacterial poisons.

Among the products of the putrefactive fermentation there are two substances which have been found to be highly irritating, viz., cadaverine and putrescine; and I have previously referred to the experiments made by Grawitz and Scheuerlen, which show that, as the result of the injection of these substances, inflammation and suppuration may occur according to the strength and quantity of the solution employed. Grawitz found further that suppuration certainly occurs, if, at the same time that a comparatively dilute solution of cadaverine is injected, pyogenic cocci are introduced.—The chemical products of the pyogenic cocci are also, according to Grawitz, irritating to the subcutaneous tissues of dogs and rabbits, when introduced in sufficient quantity and concentration. Thus he found that if sterilised cultivations of pyogenic cocci were injected in large quantities into dogs—for example, four c.c.m. of a sterilised cultivation of staphylococcus pyogenes aureus — suppuration occurred, the pus being free from organisms.

Products of the Pyogenic Organisms.—As regards the products of these pyogenic cocci, Brieger, who is the great authority on this subject, states that he has been unable as yet to obtain any toxine from the cultivations of these organisms. Cultivations of staphylococcus pyogenes aureus on moist beef or veal yield large quantities of ammonia, as does also the staphylococcus pyogenes albus; the latter produces, in addition, considerable quantities of trimethylamine. Streptococcus pyogenes likewise produces ammonia and trimethylamine. That the ammonia must irritate the tissues is of course evident, and it is probable that in the nascent state it is still more irritating ; while as regards trimethylamine, though it is not an alkaloid, it is, in Brieger's opinion, probably a descendant of, or very closely allied to, the ptomaines, and when present in considerable quantities in the body is very hurtful to it. These organisms also produce a peptonising ferment, and can thus peptonise and dissolve coagulated albumen ; and this property is, as we have seen, of great importance in suppuration. When sown in milk they rapidly set up a pure lactic fermentation, leading to the production of large quantities of lactic acid, as the result of which the milk coagulates if kept for some days at the temperature of the human body. This production of lactic acid is an important fact, as it probably also takes place sometimes in wounds, causing acidity of the discharge, and in abscesses causing the well-known watery pus. Whether ptomaines will yet be found in the case of the pyogenic cocci we cannot say, but the occurrence of fever in suppurative diseases may possibly, as Baumgarten suggests, be explained simply by the increased tissue change as the result of their growth, the products thus formed requiring increased combustion, and perhaps also stimulating the thermic centres, and hence causing elevation of temperature ; and in support of this view, Baumgarten refers to the fever which occurs in trichinosis, where there is no idea of any action of ptomaines.

Leber (*Fortschritte d. Medicin*, 1888, No. 12) states that he has isolated a crystalline substance, which he calls phlogosine, from cultivations of staphylococcus pyogenes aureus, which causes suppuration when injected into animals.

SEAT OF INOCULATION AND ANATOMICAL ARRANGEMENT
OF THE PART.

Much depends also, as regards the effect of these organisms, on the seat of inoculation and the anatomical arrangement of the part. These conditions are of importance in two ways : in the first place, certain organisms will not grow everywhere in the

5858 *SUPPURATION AND SEPTIC DISEASES.*

body, they will only grow in certain tissues; and, in the second place, in some cases, especially in the case of the pyogenic organisms, the character of the resulting disease varies chiefly according to the anatomical arrangement of the part in which the organisms are growing.

Some organisms, such as the higher fungi, seem only to be able to act if they are present within the capillary blood-vessels or large serous sacs; the bacillus of malignant œdema acts only in the cellular tissue; the micrococcus of erysipelas possibly only in the lymphatic vessels. As this is an important matter, I may refer, in some detail, to a few examples which show the great influence which these conditions exert on the development and the character of the resulting disease. In some experiments which I performed with Hauser's *proteus vulgaris,* I met at first with some very interesting difficulties. I injected the cultivations into the backs of rabbits, and I found that the results obtained varied in a manner very difficult to understand. After considerable investigation, I found that the differences depended on the seat of inoculation; that if the material was injected superficially to the muscles, a different result might be obtained to that which followed injection into the substance of the muscles. Thus quantities of a cultivation which, introduced into the subcutaneous tissue, would only have caused a large abscess, were followed, when injected into the muscles, by the death of the animal; and further, a small dose which would have been without noticeable effect on the subcutaneous tissue, was sufficient to produce an abscess when injected into the muscles. What the explanation of this difference is I am unable to say: it is possible, however, that some chemical substance in the muscle is readily broken up, and readily gives rise to poisonous compounds, and that this substance does not exist, or is present in less amount, in the subcutaneous tissue. Similar differences, according as injections were made into the subcutaneous tissue or into the muscles, were noticed in the case of several other bacteria.

Fehleisen (*Deutsch. Archiv f. klin. Chirurg. Bd.* 36, *Hft.* 4) says, that while a large quantity of staphylococcus pyogenes aureus is necessary to cause death when injected into the peritoneum, a much smaller quantity (about one-twelfth of the amount) causes suppuration in and around joints when injected into them. He also says that pus varies in virulence according to its origin, different tissues probably producing different ptomaines.

Perhaps the best example of the great influence exerted by the seat of inoculation and anatomical arrangement of the part is furnished by the disease known in this country as " Black Leg," in Germany as " Rauschbrand," and in France as " Symptomatic Anthrax." This disease has been investigated by a number of observers, chiefly by three French writers who have worked together, viz., MM. Arloing, Cornevin, and Thomas. The disease chiefly affects cattle and sheep, more especially cattle, and is characterised by the rapid appearance of irregularly limited swellings of the skin and muscular tissues, these swellings being at first very painful and tense, but rapidly becoming painless and crepitating. The disease is accompanied by fever, which is often very high, and it is almost always fatal, usually after a duration of from thirty-six to forty hours. The cause of the disease has been demonstrated to be a bacillus which grows without free oxygen, and thus belongs to Pasteur's class of anäerobes. These bacilli are remarkable in various ways, more especially in the conditions under which they exert their pathogenic action. In order to cause the death of the animal, the organisms must be introduced either into the subcutaneous tissue or into the muscles : if they are injected into the veins or into the bronchi, they do not cause the death of the animal, but apparently after a time die out, leaving the animal, however, protected against the disease. And I have already mentioned that if, after the virus has been injected into the veins, a bruise is caused in some part of the body, the organisms reach that spot from the blood, grow there, and set up the disease. If inoculations are made quite at the tip of the tail in cattle, the result is only a moderate amount of reaction, even when large quantities of the material are introduced ; the more proximal on the tail is the seat of inoculation, the more readily is a result obtained. The explanation of this fact is apparently partly the dense nature of the connective tissue at the tip of the tail, and partly also the low temperature of the part. That the density of the tissue in the tails of cattle inter- feres with the spread of the infection is evident, because sheep, at the tips of whose tails the cellular tissue is loose, react markedly on inoculation in that part. As regards the tempera- ture of the part, it has been found that if, after inoculation, the tail is wrapped in bad conductors of heat, the local temperature can be so raised that considerable reaction occurs, and *vice versa* in the case of sheep ; if, after inoculation, the part is kept cool by the application of ice-bags, the violence of the local reaction is much reduced.

As regards the pyogenic organisms, most of them act in the cellular tissue to which they gain access, as a rule, after the destruction of the epithelium. The gonococcus is, so far as we know, the only pyogenic organism in man which is able to penetrate uninjured epithelium ; and with regard to the gono- coccus, it is very striking that it only attacks certain mucous membranes, and apparently cannot develop in any other tissue of the body unless, perhaps, in the joints in which, according to Kammerer, it is present in some cases of gonorrhœal rheumatism. (It must be said, however, that other investigators have failed to confirm this observation.) Bumm states that pure gonor- rhœal pus may be injected into the subcutaneous cellular tissue without causing any reaction, and that if, after twenty- four hours, an incision is made into the part, and some of the pus which was injected is removed, it will be found that the pus cells are in good condition, but that the cocci have dis- appeared. This is a fact of great interest, as showing that pus, apart from the micro-organisms which it contains, does not exert a pyogenic action. Also, as I have previously said, when suppurative bubo occurs after gonorrhœa, the staphylococcus pyogenes aureus or albus is present in the pus from the gland and not the gonococcus, suppurative bubo being therefore the result of a mixed infection, and not a necessary complication of gonorrhœa. The same is the fact in the case of abscesses in connection with the urethra in cases of gonorrhœa.—Kitt has found that in the case of the coccus of mastitis in cows, the organisms only exert their pathogenic action when they are present in the ducts or acini of the mamma; if injected directly into the tissue of the mamma, they cause no suppuration.

Anatomical Arrangement of the Part. — The anatomical arrangement of the part is probably a very important factor in the production of acute osteo-myelitis. This disease is, as we have seen, due to the action of pyogenic cocci, and it not infrequently stands apparently in some relation to an injury. But the injury and the presence of the cocci do not explain the whole of the etiology of the disease, more especially they do not explain why it is that the disease is almost entirely limited to certain bones and to certain parts of bones. Not that most of the bones in the body may not, under certain circumstances, become the seat of this affection, but as a rule the disease has certain very favourite seats, such as the femur, especially its lower end, the upper and lower ends of the tibia, the upper end of the humerus and the radius.

It is very seldom, indeed, that the ulna, and still more seldom that the fibula is attacked.

Now, these are the bones which grow most rapidly, and in them the disease commences during the period of growth, and most usually in the neighbourhood of the epiphysial line where the growth is of course most active. Thus the fact that the bones are growing, helps apparently to determine the seat of the disease, possibly because there is a large amount of young indefinite tissue at these parts, possibly also because there are plenty of blood-vessels, and also, perhaps, because the circulation in the ends of the bone is apparently less rapid than elsewhere (Neumann). It is interesting also to note, as showing probably the influence of similar conditions, that when this disease attacks infants, it is usually limited to the neighbourhood of the epiphysial line, giving rise to acute epiphysitis. At the same time, the anatomical peculiarities will not suffice to explain all the facts, because in growing animals belonging to species not insensitive to this poison, the disease is not produced by injection into the circulation unless some other

determining cause, such as injury, comes into play; and because
also the disease not infrequently occurs after acute fevers, such
as typhoid fever.   As regards the anatomical arrangement of
the part in its relation to acute osteo-myelitis, all that we can
say, therefore, is that there is some peculiarity in growing bones
not necessarily limited to the growth at the epiphysis, which
has an important influence on the production of the disease.

The only other possible view in the cases where no injury can be made out,
would be that the disease is a specific one, and that the virus can only grow in
these situations.   This view is, however, untenable, as shown both by clinical
facts, and also by the fact that the organisms of acute osteo-myelitis are the same
as those which are present in ordinary suppuration.

Another example of the manner in which the occurrence of disease may be
influenced by the anatomical arrangement of the part is the frequency with which
pyæmia occurs after acute osteo-myelitis.   This is evidently due, in part at any
rate, to the high pressure which the pus is subjected to in the medulla of the bone,
as shown by the manner in which the fatty matter oozes out of the bone when it
is trephined, and also by the occurrence of fatty embolism in the lungs.   Just as
fatty emboli may pass into the circulation, so may emboli, consisting of groups of
cocci, or of pus containing cocci, occur.

In the case of certain organs also, it is possible that their peculiar selective
affinity for certain viruses is to a considerable extent due to the anatomical
arrangement of the part.   The great tendency of infective materials to become
located in the kidney is very striking.   I have already referred to experiments
where deposits of micrococci were found only in the kidneys, and this is also the
case with staphylococcus pyogenes aureus when injected in moderate quantities
into the veins of rabbits.   The accumulation of organisms in that organ is also
seen in the case of a number of other bacteria, and even of the higher fungi, such
as the pathogenic forms of mucor and aspergillus.   It seems to me possible that
in the case of the kidney, its excretory function may have something to do with
the tendency of organisms to accumulate in that organ.   Grawitz, however, thinks
that this selective affinity is due to differences in the energy with which different
organs assimilate nutriment, and he has constructed a scale showing the vital
energy of the various organs, and at the bottom of this scale he places the kidney.
That this is not the explanation is evident from the fact that in many cases other
organs are more frequently involved than the kidneys.   For example, in the case
of the pathogenic aspergilli in rabbits, the membranous labyrinth is apparently a
favourite seat of these fungi, and this is the explanation of the rotatory movements which are so characteristic of the affection produced by these fungi in
rabbits.   Another example of peculiar selective affinity is seen if we compare the
course of acute tuberculosis in man and in rabbits.   In man, acute general tuberculosis seldom runs its course without the occurrence of tubercular meningitis :
while in rabbits, I have never met with tubercular meningitis in the course of
a large number of inoculation experiments.

I have also said that as the result of differences in the seat
of inoculation and the anatomical arrangement of the part,
there may be differences in the character of the disease pro-

duced. Virchow has long ago pointed out that the cause of
a disease does not by any means determine the product of the
disease, for that depends chiefly on the internal predisposition:
thus the same agent acting on the cellular tissue may cause
thickening of it, and acting on the periosteum, may lead to new
formation of bone. This is probably a great part of the explanation of the different types of disease produced by these pyogenic
organisms, according as they act in the skin or in the connective tissue. I have previously mentioned the result of Bockhardt's investigations on impetigo and boil, from which it is
evident that the character of the inflammation depends greatly
on the point of entrance and the seat of development of the
organisms, and Garré also comes to the same conclusion. It
seems that in the case of multiple abscesses of the skin in infants,
the cocci also spread into the hair follicles and sebaceous and
sweat glands, and growing there, set up inflammation and
abscess, the process being similar to that which occurs in the
formation of boils in adults, but being clinically distinguished
from that by the tendency to form true abscesses, and by the
absence of necrosis. Escherich believes that these differences
depend on differences in the degree of tension of the skin in
adults and infants, more especially in atrophic infants, in which
these abscesses are especially apt to occur. It is possible,
however, that, as Baumgarten points out, the greater softness
and irritability of the tissues of the child as compared with
those of the adult, play an important part.

The different course which is run by acute osteo-myelitis
when it occurs spontaneously, and when it follows operations on
bones, is also probably due, in the main, to the seat of inoculation. In the latter case, we never see the scattered patches
of necrosis which so frequently occur in the former, and this may
be explained by the fact that, in the latter, the infective agents
spread continuously in the tissue from the point of inoculation,
whereas in the former they are carried by the blood and may
be deposited at various parts, thus giving rise to various foci of
disease.

LECTURE III.

Suppurative Peritonitis.—Another example of the influence
of the seat of inoculation and the anatomical arrangement of
the part is the difference in the behaviour of the peritoneum as
compared with the cellular tissue in regard to the pyogenic
organisms. In former times the peritoneal cavity was looked
on as one especially liable to inflame, and it was thought to be
one of the chief triumphs of antiseptic surgery that operations
could be performed on the peritoneum without bad result. The
experience of a number of surgeons, however, has now shown
that it is not absolutely necessary for success in operations on
the peritoneal cavity that all bacteria should be excluded; in
fact, this seems to be much less necessary than where operations
are performed on other serous cavities, such as joints, or on the
subcutaneous or muscular tissues.

The explanation of this surprising result is found in the
nature of the lining wall of the cavity, and in the conditions
under which pyogenic organisms find themselves there. The
peritoneum has marvellous powers of absorbing fluids, and thus
effusions into it are very rapidly removed, and in this way
micro-organisms are deprived of the necessary nutrient material,
while they are also in all probability absorbed along with the
fluid, and destroyed in the blood or excreted. Wegner, who

performed a number of experiments on this subject some years ago, has shown in a very striking manner the great absorptive power of the peritoneum. I may mention one of his experiments: 200 c.c.m. of warm serum were injected in the peritoneal cavity of a rabbit, an hour later the animal was bled to death, and the amount of fluid then present in the peritoneal cavity was only 66 c.c.m., no less than 134 c.c.m. having been absorbed in one hour.—Apparently the rapidity of absorption of fluid depends, in the first place, to a great extent on the tension under which the fluid is, fluid under low tension, as when the walls of the abdomen are lax, or the fluid itself is small in amount, being absorbed comparatively slowly; and in the second place on the nature of the fluid, fluid of lower specific gravity than blood serum, leading in the first instance to transudation from the blood. If we contrast with this the condition of a wound in the cellular or muscular tissues in respect of its absorptive power, we find that we have not here an actively absorbing surface; in fact, the whole surface is for a few hours in the early stage of inflammation, as the result of the injury done by the knife, and is not only not an absorbing surface, but is not even a healthy surface.

Wegner has also shown that a great variety of fluids free from bacteria, such as water, bile, urine, blood, &c., may be injected into the peritoneal cavity of rabbits without causing any bad results, and even large quantities of unfiltered air may be similarly introduced without setting up peritonitis, the air being soon absorbed, though by no means so rapidly as fluids. If putrescible fluids are injected into the peritoneal cavity at the same time that air is introduced, they rapidly undergo decomposition, but this is only the case if the quantity of fluid is too great to be quickly absorbed. Thus 15 c.c.m. of putrescible fluid injected into the peritoneal cavity of a rabbit will usually be absorbed before decomposition has had time to occur, but if as much as 50 c.c.m. are employed, then only a part is taken up during the first hour, and the rest furnishes a substratum for the growth of the organisms present in the injected air, and these organisms develop with extraordinary

E

rapidity, and may cause the death of the animal from septic intoxication.

In none of Wegner's experiments with the injection of putrefying or putrescible fluids and air, did peritonitis occur, and Grawitz, who has since investigated the matter, has directed special attention to the conditions under which peritonitis is produced. Apparently the explanation why Wegner did not obtain peritonitis, but only septic intoxication, is that pyogenic organisms are not frequently present in the air, and were therefore not injected along with it, and also that they only act under certain special conditions.

As the result of Grawitz's experiments, the following seem to be the facts of the case. In the first place, saprophytic bacteria are absorbed or destroyed by the peritoneum in relatively enormous numbers; where, however, the peritoneum is abnormal, or where the bacteria are able to set up putrefaction, the symptoms of septic intoxication as described by Wegner result, but these symptoms are unaccompanied by suppurative peritonitis. In the second place, pyogenic organisms, when injected in small numbers into the normal peritoneal cavity, and when suspended in such an amount of indifferent fluid as can be readily absorbed, cause no peritonitis; but, on the other hand, peritonitis occurs as the result of the injection of these organisms if the peritoneum is abnormal, or, if with a normal peritoneum, large numbers of pyogenic cocci are introduced, or if the cocci are suspended in too large an amount of fluid to be quickly absorbed. The necessary abnormal conditions of the peritoneum may be set up, if at the same time that the pyogenic organisms are introduced, substances act which weaken or kill the tissue of the peritoneum, and thus provide a suitable soil for the penetration of the cocci; and above all, if there is a wound of the peritoneal wall in which the infective organisms can develop.

The factors, then, which are required to produce suppurative peritonitis are—the presence of the pyogenic cocci, usually the streptococcus pyogenes, along with too large an amount of fluid to be rapidly absorbed, or along with disease of the peritoneum, or themselves in too large numbers, or acting in too great concentration. In other words, to develop suppurative peritonitis, the cocci must either be introduced in such numbers along with their products, that a part of the peritoneum is at once injured, and thus ceases to exercise its normal functions; or they must be introduced into an unhealthy peritoneum, or they must be able to grow in the peritoneal cavity, either because fluid is present in too large a quantity to be quickly absorbed, or because the absorptive power of the peritoneum has been diminished, or because some material, such as a piece of blood clot, or a piece of injured or dead tissue, is present, in which they can develop.

Suppurative peritonitis occurs with the greatest certainty where there is a wound of the abdominal wall, in which the infective agents can develop, and which forms a centre from which organisms are constantly given off into the cavity, and from which the organisms can spread in the tissue of the peritoneum. It is still more certain to occur if the wound is an unhealthy one. This is well exemplified by the difference in the result of operations for rupture of healthy intestine, and for perforation in typhoid fever for example. In the rupture of healthy bowel, if the extravasated contents are thoroughly removed from the peritoneal cavity, and the wound stitched early, recovery frequently occurs. In perforation, after ulceration of the bowel, the wall of the hole is unhealthy, and forms a nidus in which the organisms grow, and the only chance of success in such a case is resection of the portion of bowel involved. The danger of peritonitis after perforation depends (1), on the nature of the materials extravasated into the peritoneal cavity; (2), on their quantity; and (3), on the previous existence of ulceration of the coats of the ruptured viscus.

It is evident, therefore, that when surgeons draw conclusions to the effect that aseptic treatment is unnecessary in surgical practice, because they obtain good results in operations on the peritoneum when they take care to introduce as few of these organisms as possible,—in many cases, probably, none at all are introduced,—to introduce them in as dilute a state as possible, to remove all the fluid and other materials, such as blood clot, in which they can grow, and to avoid injury to the peritoneum, as far as they can, they make an assumption which is not at all in accord with other clinical and experimental observations. The points which I have mentioned amply explain the results, and bring them into unison with those of experiments and of clinical experience with regard to other tissues of the body.

It is an equally erroneous assumption that because good results may be got in peritoneal surgery in this way, it is therefore the right method of treatment to adopt. The good results thus obtained depend, to a great extent, on chance, and are only got with a great deal of trouble. Surely, seeing that by destroying the organisms before they enter the body the element of chance is abolished without any harm to the patient, and with less trouble to the operator, it must be very wrong to subject the patient to an unnecessary, even though possibly a small risk. And, besides, it is only a surgeon of large experience who can get good results in these cases without aseptic treatment, while the employment of that treatment puts it in the power of any reasonably qualified surgeon to obtain equally good and even better, results.

INDEFINITE CONDITIONS ON THE PART OF THE BODY.

We have also to consider conditions of a more indefinite character on the part of the body. Thus :—

Age, as we have seen, is an important factor in the production of acute osteo-myelitis. This is a disease of youth, and occurs most frequently between the ages of seven and twenty, and I have mentioned the different situations which are attacked in infants and in youths. Other diseases also vary in frequency at different ages ; thus spontaneous erysipelas is apparently most frequent in persons between thirty-five and forty-five years of age, and next most frequent between forty-five and fifty-five. Diphtheria most commonly occurs below five years of age, and steadily decreases in frequency as the patients grow older.

Sex.—As regards sex also, we find in some of these diseases a marked difference in the frequency of occurrence in the two sexes ; thus spontaneous erysipelas is apparently much more frequent in women than in men. Eschbaum found in 181 cases, that 122 of those attacked were females, and only 59 were males. Osteo-myelitis is, as we have seen, most common in males.

State of the Digestive Organs.—It is possible that the state of the digestive organs may have an important influence on the occurrence of these suppurative diseases, as shown by Kocher's experiments and views on the production of acute osteo-myelitis.

Kocher came to the conclusion, in the case of dogs, that after injury to bone this disease could be induced by feeding the animals with large quantities of putrid materials; and he thinks that in many cases of acute osteo-myelitis, the starting-point is a disturbance of the digestive organs, permitting excessive multiplication of bacteria in the intestinal canal, and their entrance into the blood. In fact, Kocher holds that an individual in whose intestinal canal fermentative changes of an intense character are going on, is practically in the incubation stage of acute suppurative inflammation, which will then develop if an injury or some other local depressing cause comes into play. In this way Kocher explains the occurrence of acute osteo-myelitis after typhoid fever, and he relates a case observed by Kappeler as bearing on this view, in which a girl, shortly after recovery from an attack of epidemic cholerine, knelt for a long time in church, and was immediately afterwards attacked with acute osteo-myelitis of the tibia. Kraske, however, who has paid great attention to this matter in *post-mortem* examinations of cases of acute osteo-myelitis, and has carefully examined the wall of the intestine and the mesenteric glands, both microscopically and by cultivation, states that he has never been able to obtain any evidence that the infective material had entered the body by these channels. Whether Kocher's view is correct or not, the possibility that during the progress of some wound or inflammatory disease, if the digestive organs are very much out of order, organisms may multiply to a great extent in the intestinal canal, and may enter the blood, and thus reach the seat of the local disease or injury, is worth bearing in mind.

Diet.—It is possible also that the nature of the diet may affect the occurrence of these diseases. In has been observed, for instance, in the case of symptomatic anthrax, that calves are more or less immune against this disease so long as they are fed on milk; but that after this period has passed, and when their diet becomes exclusively vegetable, they lose their immunity. Arloing, Cornevin, and Thomas explain this by supposing that the milk diet induces a particular constitution of the body,

which is unfavourable to the development of this disease; but
on the other hand, this may be a mere coincidence, and the
cause may be some peculiarity in the youthful connective tissue.

State of the Blood—Diabetes.—The state of the blood is also
of importance; for example, the frequency of carbuncle and
furuncle, and of ulcerative and suppurative affections, and their
stubborn course in cases of diabetes is well known. It is very
probable that part of the explanation of this fact is the presence
of the sugar or its chemical progenitors in the juices of the part,
leading to the formation of a better pabulum for the development of the micro-organisms; though, no doubt, much depends
on what we must more vaguely term the general depression of
vitality of the tissues, caused by the disease.

Since the above was written, Bujwid (*Centralblatt für Bakteriologie, &c.*, vol.
iv., p. 577) has investigated this point, and has found that the second hypothesis is
the correct one. He first ascertained that the pyogenic staphylococci did not grow
so well in nutrient media, containing 5 per cent. of grape sugar, as in the ordinary
material. He then ascertained the number of these cocci required to do harm
when injected subcutaneously, and he estimates them at more than one billion in
rabbits. If, however, they were mixed with a fluid containing 25 per cent. of
grape sugar, one billion caused a large abscess; while, without the sugar, the
same quantity produced no effect. Again, if about 500,000 cocci were injected in
a fluid containing 12 per cent of grape sugar, they did no harm; but if in another
animal the same quantity was injected, and a 12 per cent. solution of grape sugar
was also injected daily at the same spot, an abscess formed. The daily injection
of the grape sugar alone did not cause abscess, nor did abscess occur if three days
elapsed before the second injection, *i.e.*, if time were given for the staphylococci to
be destroyed. The injection of ten syringefuls of a 10 per cent. solution of grape
sugar into the veins, and of one billion cocci subcutaneously at the same time,
led to gangrene of the skin at the seat of the injection.—These experiments were
repeated and confirmed by Karlinski, and they show that the presence of grape
sugar in the tissues so depresses their vitality, that the pyogenic cocci can act in
much smaller numbers and more vigorously than would otherwise be the case.

Dilution of the Blood also apparently interferes, to some
extent, though only slightly, with the rapidity with which
bacteria are killed in it. Thus Von Fodor found that if at the
same time that non-pathogenic bacteria were injected, a quantity
of water was introduced into the blood, the bacteria did not
disappear so quickly as in undiluted blood. Pettenkofer, in fact,
has come to the conclusion that everything which increases the

amount of water in the body, increases the predisposition of the individual to infective diseases.

Albuminuria.—There is no doubt, also, that other chronic affections, such as albuminuria, predispose to septic diseases.

Acute Diseases, such as acute fevers, also predispose to these affections, as in the case of the occurrence of acute osteomyelitis after acute fevers, of pneumonia after typhoid fever, &c.; probably in part, because, as in the case of scarlet fever, the pyogenic organisms are able to enter and live in the blood.

Tension apparently has a considerable influence in causing inflammation, and in predisposing to suppuration. The spread of an abscess after it has once completely formed, is no doubt largely due to the tension of its contents, for the microscopical examination of the wall shows that the increase is not due, after a time, to the spread of the organisms in the tissues ; and also if an abscess is opened aseptically and well drained, the secretion of pus ceases. The same is seen in the case of wounds, where, if micro-organisms are present, the occurrence of tension from accumulation of discharge, is apt to be followed by suppuration, and where, on relief of the tension, the suppuration ceases.

I have more than once observed in abscesses which had been opened aseptically, that when the drainage tube had become blocked, or had slipped out, the retained fluid was clear serum and not pus, if it was let out in the course of twenty-four or forty-eight hours.

Lessening of Predisposition.—In some cases, however, the predisposition is apparently lessened as the result of the action of various indeterminate causes; and apparently, also, this lessening of the predisposition may be due to a previous attack of the same disease, though, as regards the organisms under consideration, erysipelas seems to be the only case where a temporary and partial protection is attained.

CONDITIONS ON THE PART OF THE BACTERIA.

We now come to the consideration of the conditions which more especially affect the bacteria, and which are not perhaps

of less importance than those to which we have been alluding;
these are chiefly the species, the dose and concentration of the
organisms, the virulence, and the concurrent growth with other
bacteria.

INFLUENCE OF SPECIES.

As regards the species, while, as we have said before,
the nature of a disease does not by any means altogether
depend on its cause, it does so to a very large extent; and all
writers are now agreed as to differences in the pathogenic
action of the pyogenic streptococci and staphylococci. These
differences have been previously referred to, and it has been
seen that the streptococci are generally associated with erysipe-
latoid processes, while the staphylococci tend to cause more
circumscribed suppurations. The streptococcus is by far the
most dangerous organism, and apparently has the property
of creeping in the living tissue, spreading in it for a time
without being noticed, and then setting up violent reaction.
Fraenkel has found streptococcus pyogenes in a great variety
of puerperal diseases, especially in the so-called lymphangoitic
forms. It gains entrance to the cellular tissue of the pelvis
from ulcers in the vagina, spreads in the pelvic cellular tissue,
reaches the ligamenta lata and the peritoneum, and spreading
along the lymphatic channels, ultimately attacks the diaphragm
and pleura; finally it reaches the blood, and causes septicæmia,
pyæmia, suppuration in joints, &c. As regards the other
pyogenic cocci, I have already referred to the differences in
their effects on animals, some of them not being pathogenic in
rabbits, and some, such as micrococcus pyogenes tenuis, being
especially associated in man with mild inflammations.

In acute osteo-myelitis it is almost always staphylococci that are present
though it is possible that streptococci may also cause it. Although this fact
cannot be used as an absolute diagnostic sign, nevertheless it is of great value. If
streptococcus is found, say in a suppurating knee joint, the probabilities in favour
of osteo-myelitis are less than if staphylococcus is present; and in one case of this
kind, Krause made the diagnosis of the absence of osteo-myelitis from the presence
of streptococci in a suppurating knee joint, a diagnosis fully confirmed by *post-
mortem* examination.

DOSE AND CONCENTRATION OF THE ORGANISMS.

Perhaps the most important factor on the part of the micro-organisms is the dose or number, and the concentration in which they enter the body. Ogston has already laid stress on the dose, as explaining the different diseases which result from the introduction of these organisms, and he looks on the difference between acute abscess and pyæmia as in the main a quantitative one. This, however, is only partially correct, as must now be evident.

Various authors have, from time to time, mentioned with regard to bacteria, that some act best or only when present in large numbers, but the matter has not till recently been thoroughly worked out. I was led to investigate this matter in connection with some interesting experiments made by Sir Joseph Lister, which appeared to show that one or a few putrefactive bacteria could not set up putrefaction in blood taken with various antiseptic precautions, while that result was obtained if a mass of putrefying material was added to it. At first sight I did not think that it could matter much, except as regards the rapidity of the result, whether, to begin with, one or a million bacteria were employed; but, nevertheless, I determined to put the matter to the proof, and, to my surprise, I found that difference in dose was a most important factor in the production and the type of many diseases. The experiments were made in such a manner that I was able to ascertain exactly the number of bacteria introduced, the material being, in the first place, diluted to such an extent that, on a rough estimation with the microscope, I obtained a general idea as to the number of bacteria present in a given quantity of the fluid; a known amount of this fluid was then injected into the animals, and at the same time a measured quantity was thoroughly mixed with liquefied nutrient jelly, which was then poured out on glass plates and allowed to solidify. By counting the number of colonies of bacteria which developed on these plates, each colony probably originating from a single bacterium, I ascertained exactly how many organisms were present in the amount of fluid injected.

Experiments with Proteus vulgaris. —Without going into further details, the following are the most important results that I obtained. In the case of Hauser's *proteus vulgaris*, I found that a definite and large dose of the cultivation in nutrient jelly was necessary to kill rabbits, and in comparing these doses I took care that they were always injected into the same tissue, *e.g.*, the muscles, in accordance with the facts previously mentioned with regard to the importance of the seat of inoculation. I found that about 1-10th c.c.m. of an undiluted cultivation was a rapidly fatal dose when injected into the muscles, and I ascertained that this quantity contained about 225 millions of bacteria; 1-40th c.c.m., containing therefore about 56,000,000 bacteria, always caused an extensive abscess, of which the animals usually died in six to eight weeks. Doses of less than 1-500th c.c.m. produced no effect, in fact, doses of less than 1-120th c.c.m., or in other words, fewer than 18,000,000 bacteria seldom caused any result. From 1-120th to 1-40th c.c.m. caused abscesses, above 1-20 c.c.m. caused death in twenty-four to thirty-six hours. Further, the size of the abscess apparently depended on the initial dose. If 1-500th c.c.m. caused any effect at all, it was only a slight trace of whiteness in the tissues which soon disappeared, while 1-40th c.c.m. caused a large and spreading abscess, ultimately resulting in the death of the animal, and intermediate doses produced abscesses intermediate in size. Further, the *concentration* of the bacteric material is also of great importance, as shown by the fact that the dose must act at the same place at the same time. It apparently will not do to split up the dose and inject various portions of it into different parts of the same animal at successive periods of time, or even at the same time. In both cases the effect of the smaller dose is produced.

Experiments with the bacilli of mouse septicæmia. —I have tested this matter in the case of a number of other infective diseases, and have found that the result depended mainly on what we may, for want of better knowledge, term the predisposition of the animal to the disease. Thus, in the case of mouse septicæmia, mice, which are extremely susceptible to this disease, die as the result of the injection of a single bacillus; while the only result of the injection of 4 c.c.m. of a jelly cultivation containing myriads of bacilli into the base of the ear of rabbits, is to cause illness for a few days, along with slight swelling and redness of the part.

Experiments with Chicken Cholera.—In like manner, in the case of chicken cholera, rabbits die apparently as the result of the introduction of a single microbe, but a considerable number —somewhere between 150,000 and 300,000—are required to cause the death of a guinea pig; and here again we meet with the fact that where the animal is less predisposed to the disease, we have different effects, according to differences in the dose. As I have said, 300,000 bacilli are apparently able to kill guinea pigs; as the result of a smaller dose, down to 10,000, abscesses form, while with less than 10,000 bacilli, apparently no effect is produced.

Experiments with Pyogenic Cocci.—In the case of staphylococcus pyogenes aureus, I have found that it was necessary to inject something like 1,000,000,000 cocci into the muscles of rabbits, in order to cause the death of the animal, while 250,000,000 produced a small circumscribed abscess. The same result was obtained with staphylococcus pyogenes albus, only apparently fewer cocci were required.

This is no doubt a large number, and does not say much for the pathogenic power of these organisms in rabbits. There is no doubt, however, that man is very much more susceptible to the staphylococci than rabbits, and consequently a very much smaller number will produce the same result in man. Besides, in the above experiments, there was no weak spot, and therefore all the conditions were unfavourable for their growth. Usually, however, in man there is a weak spot, and consequently the requisite dose is still smaller.—These numbers apply to injection into the muscles ; where the injection is into the subcutaneous tissues, much larger quantities are necessary to produce the same results.

Experiments with the Tetanus Bacillus.—In the case of the tetanus bacillus, death did not occur in rabbits when fewer than 1000 bacilli were introduced.

Explanation of these Results.—I think that in these experiments a good deal depends on the simultaneous action of the products of the bacteria, and I would suggest the following explanation of the facts. When the animals are not very susceptible to the action of a bacterium, the cells and tissues soon gain the victory in the struggle for existence, but where a large number of bacteria are introduced at one place, they grow for a time before they are attacked by the cells, and growing there, each produces a small quantity of poisonous material. The products thus formed must interfere with the action of the cells, and thus enable the bacteria to gain a foothold. The greater the number of the bacteria introduced at one time, the greater will be the amount of these products, the more extensive the foothold, and the more marked the result. Where only one or a few bacteria are introduced into a slightly susceptible animal, they are overpowered by the cells and quickly destroyed. When the number of bacteria is greater, these poisonous products destroy the tissue in their vicinity, and enable the bacteria to spread over a large area before the cells collecting around them are able to form an efficient barrier against their progress; and where the dose is very large, no efficient barrier can be set up in time, and the death of the animal is the result. Thus the extent to which the organisms spread, and the violence of their action in animals not very susceptible to the disease, depends firstly on the number of bacteria and the quantity of products introduced in the first instance, and secondly, on the vitality of the animal and the rapidity with which a granulation wall is formed.

Laws deduced from these Results.—The facts made out in this research enabled me to lay down the following laws:— In the first place, *the pathogenic dose of a virus varies inversely with the predisposition of the animal to the disease in question;* the greater the predisposition the less is the quantity required, and conversely the less the predisposition the greater is the number of bacteria that must be introduced to produce the same effect. Of course the term "predisposition" is an absolutely indefinite one, but I have already discussed a number of conditions which go together to make up predisposition, and it is a convenient term as expressing a complex set of conditions, which undoubtedly exist, but about which we do not know very much.—A second law is that *in animals which are not very susceptible to a disease, the severity of the affection varies directly within certain limits with the amount of virus introduced.* In all the affections of this class which I have investigated, I found three stages according to the quantity of virus injected: firstly, a stage, where with a small dose no apparent effect was produced; secondly, an intermediate stage, where a local affection resulted, the extent of the local affection depending to a great degree on the dose of the virus; and thirdly, a stage where, after a very large dose, death occurred. Of course, as predisposition varies in the same species of animal—for example in man—we cannot measure out the dose, nor calculate the effects of a given dose in each instance.

The importance of these facts as regards dose is very great in connection with our subject, for man is not very susceptible to the action of pyogenic organisms, and the results produced by them vary to a great extent in accordance with the second law. In the case of wounds, it is important to know that apparently in man a single pyogenic coccus might possibly do no harm, unless, indeed, it met with conditions, such as retention of fluid, under which it could grow. At the same time, I doubt whether a single coccus ever enters a wound; as a rule, they occur in masses containing many cocci, and then of course we have the effects of a large dose. And further, there is no doubt that man is very much more susceptible to the action of these organisms than rabbits, and therefore a very much smaller dose will probably produce the same effect. The facts as regards dose probably explain to some extent the fairly good results obtained where, by imperfect attempts at antiseptic work, the introduction of gross particles of dirt, that is to say, of large numbers of organisms, is avoided, and where consequently the effect of the injection of a small instead of a large dose of a virus is obtained.

The importance of dose has, as I have said before, been mentioned by various observers. Thus Ribbert, in his research on experimental myocarditis and endocarditis already referred to, found that in order to obtain the desired result, it was necessary to inject a considerable quantity of the cultivations. Thus a Pravaz syringeful of the emulsion killed the animals in from twenty to twenty-four hours; if the dose was somewhat less, the animals might live even for five days; if only one-sixth of a syringeful was injected, the animals lived still longer, and endocarditis was not produced. In the case of symptomatic anthrax, the relation of dose to the production of disease is extremely marked, a small dose either producing no effect at all, or only local reaction, which, however, may suffice to render the animal immune; while a larger dose causes the death of the animal.

VIRULENCE.

It is also important to remember that organisms may vary in virulence at different times, and that the greater the virulence of the organisms, the less are other conditions necessary to enable them to gain a foothold. A virus (or at any rate most viruses) is, as regards virulence, not a fixed quantity; it is, in fact, in a constant state of variation, under the influence of the external conditions under which it finds itself. I need not refer to the well-known facts with regard to variations in virulence in the case of anthrax, chicken cholera, swine erysipelas, &c., as the result of variations in the mode of cultivation outside the body; but I may mention some of the points which seem to bear especially on the pyogenic organisms. In many cases it is found that, as the cultivations carried on outside the body become older, so the virulence of the organisms is apt to decrease. This is very well seen in the case of Fraenkel's pneumonia coccus, which loses its virulence within two or three days when grown in the same medium outside the body, and which, if its virulence is to be maintained, must be re-inoculated frequently, and passed from time to time through the animal body. It can be readily seen, also, that staphylococcus pyogenes aureus grows most luxuriantly in the early cultivations from the body, but after it has been artificially cultivated for some time, its growth is by no means so rapid. Emmerich states, with regard to cultivations of erysipelas cocci, that they vary much in virulence, and that the longer the time between each fresh inoculation, the less is the virulence of the culture; in fact, the erysipelas cocci can be readily attenuated to such a degree, that they can no longer kill mice.

It is important, also, to remember that where the virulence of an organism is diminished, its effects on animals vary in accordance with the second law; thus, if a considerable number of attenuated anthrax bacilli are injected into rabbits, the result will be, not a general fatal disease, but a local inflammatory affection, with possibly the production of an abscess, varying in size to a certain extent with the amount of virus injected. In fact, the effect of the attenuated organisms on animals highly susceptible to the virulent virus, is the same as if virulent organisms were injected into less susceptible animals; and, consequently, in order to produce the same effect as with the virulent organisms, correspondingly large doses of the attenuated organisms are required. Thus Kitt and Hueppe have found that they could obtain the same result by injection of the organisms of an infective disease of deer into animals, if, as the organisms lost their virulence, they increased the number of microbes injected. These facts are also important as showing how, even in a mild epidemic of a disease, where the virulence of the virus is not very great, bad cases may occur where extra large doses of the virus have been taken in, and this is probably in part the explanation of the occurrence of isolated severe cases in the course of a mild epidemic.

It is further important to note that loss of virulence may not only be due to the ordinary conditions of growth, but may also result from the action of various chemical substances. Thus carbolic acid and other antiseptics apparently diminish the virulence of anthrax bacilli, and it is possible that something of the same kind occurs with regard to the pyogenic cocci in wounds; and this may to some extent explain why, at the present day, although pyogenic cocci occasionally enter wounds treated aseptically, they sometimes do but little harm, less harm, in fact, than when they enter wounds in the treatment of which these antiseptics are not employed. It is quite possible that in growing in fluids containing a minute amount of an antiseptic, they are deprived, at any rate to some extent, of their virulence.

Increase in Virulence.—As regards increase of virulence, a very curious observation has been made in reference to the bacilli of symptomatic anthrax. It has been found that the addition of a minute quantity of lactic acid to a fluid containing these bacilli, increases the virulence of a very attenuated virus within a very short time. Thus Arloing, Cornevin, and Thomas found that if to a fluid containing these bacilli 1-500th part of lactic acid is added, and the mixture allowed to stand for twenty-four hours, the pathogenic power is increased two-fold ; if, then, a little water containing a very easily fermentescible sugar is added to the mixture, and another twenty-four hours allowed to elapse, the virulence has attained its maximum ; and frogs inoculated with this virus die in from twelve to fifteen hours, whereas, when inoculated with ordinary virus, they live forty to fifty hours. Kitt has repeated and confirmed these experiments, and he mentions the following :—A small quantity of the vaccine material, *i.e.*, the attenuated virus of symptomatic anthrax, was divided into two parts, of which one was mixed with water and injected into two guinea-pigs, while the other was mixed with the same quantity of water to which three drops of lactic acid had been added ; this mixture, after standing for six hours, was injected into the other two guinea-pigs. The result was that the first two guinea-pigs remained well, the virus being very attenuated, while the last two guinea-pigs died of typical symptomatic anthrax within twenty-four hours. With regard to this point, it is worthy of note that the pyogenic cocci when grown in milk, for example, produce lactic acid ; but, so far as I am aware, there is no evidence that under these circumstances their virulence is altered. Something of this kind may, however, be the explanation of Ogston's results; he found that if pyogenic cocci were grown in eggs, their virulence was increased, and he attributed this result to the absence of oxygen. I tested this matter, with regard to the possible alteration in virulence when grown in various gases, without being able to make out any noticeable difference; but it may be that, in Ogston's experiments, some chemical substance was present in the egg, or was produced by the organisms when growing in that material, which led to the increase in virulence. The fact with regard to lactic acid does not apply to the coccus of pneumonia, which, according to A. Fraenkel, loses its virulence most quickly when grown in milk, and, in his opinion, this is due to the presence of lactic acid produced by this organism. Whether or not this fact has any bearing on our subject, it is worth remembering, as showing what slight and unexpected causes may alter the virulence, and thus cause a difference in the result of the action of these organisms.

Virulence may also be increased or diminished by passing the organisms through certain animals. Thus, according to Pasteur, the bacilli of swine erysipelas are weakened by passing through rabbits, and strengthened by passing through pigeons ; and according to Arloing, Cornevin, and Thomas, Rauschbrand bacilli may be strengthened by passing through quite young guinea-pigs (one to three days old). It is quite possible that something of the same kind may happen in the case of the pyogenic or erysipelas cocci, and that they may leave certain individuals in a more or less virulent condition than when they entered them.

CONCURRENT GROWTH WITH OTHER BACTERIA.

We have also to consider the effect of the concurrent growth with other bacteria, and we shall find that the result may be either to increase or diminish the pathogenic action; in man, in all probability, the pathogenic action of the pyogenic organisms is generally increased. When two organisms grow together in the same medium outside the body, they either do not interfere with each other, or, what perhaps most frequently happens, one of them gains the upper hand in the struggle for existence, and if a number of bacteria gain access to a wound, a struggle for the mastery at once commences between the different kinds. In wounds this struggle, in most cases, probably results in

F

favour of the pyogenic cocci, and as the result of the concurrent growth other factors come into play which still further
aid their action.

As a rule, the foul smell of a wound is greatest within a few days after it has
been made, and it generally decreases as time goes on, especially if the drainage is
good : in other words, the putrefactive bacteria gradually cease to exert their
action.

Thus, although the pyogenic cocci gain the upper hand, the
putrefactive bacteria may aid their action very much, for the
products of putrefaction when absorbed act in an extremely
poisonous manner, depress the vitality of the patient, and may
thus enable the cocci to live in the body; and locally these
products injure the young granulation tissue of the wound, and
thus may open up an entrance for the pyogenic organisms. I
have already referred to the experiments made by Grawitz and
Scheuerlen on cadaverine and putrescine, and it will be remem-
bered that these experiments showed that these substances,
when present along with the pyogenic cocci, enabled the latter
to obtain a foothold in the body. The bad effects resulting
from the concurrent growth of different kinds of bacteria are
also very evident in tubercular cases. If a sinus leading to
carious bone, the wall of which is lined with tubercles containing tubercle bacilli, becomes the seat of development of these
pyogenic cocci, the result may be—in fact, generally is—a more
rapid growth of the tubercle bacilli; and it seems that it is just
in these septic cases, especially where irritating injections are
also employed, that the danger of further and general tubercular
infection is greatest; the local depression of vitality produced
by the septic organisms enabling the tubercle bacilli to grow
more luxuriantly.

Mixed Infection.—Then also, in some instances, it appears
that a mixed infection is more dangerous than infection with
one species of organism. Thus, in some cases, the presence of
more than one kind of pyogenic organism apparently increases
the severity of the suppurative process. Kraske, for example,
has observed in acute osteo-myelitis that the cases were most

severe when the infection was a mixed one—that is to say, when the disease was caused not only by the staphylococcus pyogenes aureus, but where in addition albus, and in some cases the streptococcus pyogenes were also present; and as a result of his observations he thinks that the discovery of mixed infection in acute osteo-myelitis ought to lead to a bad prognosis. Probably also one reason why we so seldom at the present day see the extremely bad septic cases formerly described is that, even where the treatment is not thoroughly aseptic, such precautions are taken as to exclude not only gross masses of dirt, in other words large numbers of the organisms, but also a great mixture of them. And this is possibly also, in part, the reason why, in my first work on this subject, I was led to think that bacilli were of more importance in wounds than micrococci, for I observed that the wounds in which both organisms were present did not pursue so favourable a course as where the cocci alone were found.

Antagonism of certain Bacteria.—Apparently, however, in some cases the presence of two species of pathogenic organisms is better for the animal than if only one species is present, and although the facts as yet made out have no direct bearing on the production of suppuration, yet, as they are of great interest, and as something similar may occur in the case of the pyogenic cocci, I shall mention some of the experiments. A number of observers have attempted to utilise the antagonism which exists between certain species of bacteria in cultivations outside the body as a means of cure when the body is attacked by organisms, but till quite recently these attempts have not been followed by success. Emmerich, however, has lately performed some very remarkable experiments on rabbits, showing the value of the erysipelas cocci as a protective and curative agent in these animals; for example, in one set of experiments rabbits were first inoculated with large numbers of the cocci of erysipelas, and then two to fourteen days later anthrax bacilli were introduced. Of fifteen animals treated in this way seven recovered, while all the control animals inoculated with anthrax

alone died; of the seven animals which died after inoculation
of both organisms some succumbed to the anthrax bacillus and
some to the erysipelas organism. The results were not so
successful when, after anthrax had been set up, and after
symptoms of disease had appeared, erysipelas cocci were injected
subcutaneously, but they were somewhat better when the erysipelas cocci were injected into the blood stream.

In one set of experiments anthrax was first induced in sixteen animals, and
when the symptoms of the disease had appeared erysipelas cocci were injected
subcutaneously. Of these only two recovered. In three sets of experiments where
half a million anthrax bacilli were injected into each animal, and where subsequently erysipelas cocci were introduced into the veins, the animals thus treated
recovered, though after a long illness ; while those kept for control, without the
injection of the erysipelas cocci, all died.

In a later paper Emmerich and Mattei communicated
results obtained by injecting erysipelas cocci into the circulation and subcutaneously in rabbits about twenty-four hours
before infection with anthrax. They found that in rabbits in
whose bodies large numbers of erysipelas cocci were present,
anthrax bacilli, though injected in enormous numbers, were
destroyed in from twelve to seventeen hours, and could not be
found either at the seat of injection or in the blood and internal
organs, whether by microscopical examination or by cultivation ;
the bacilli were evidently unable to penetrate into the blood
and internal organs, nor could they cause any local reaction or
œdema, in fact, they very quickly died out. Perhaps still more
remarkable are the experiments performed by Pawlowski. He
found that after injection of a mixture of erysipelas cocci and
pure cultivations of anthrax bacilli under the skin of seven
rabbits only two died. Pawlowski has also made the important
discovery that the erysipelas coccus is not the only organism
which interferes with the growth of anthrax in the body. Thus
ten rabbits were first inoculated with anthrax bacilli and then
cultivations of micrococcus prodigiosus were injected subcutaneously into each animal on two occasions, two and twenty-four
hours after infection; of these ten animals eight recovered.
He also found that subcutaneous injection of anthrax bacilli
and cultivations of the pneumonia cocci was not fatal to rabbits.

and that subcutaneous injection of cultivations of anthrax bacilli and staphylococcus pyogenes aureus was not followed by the death of the animal; four rabbits treated in this way recovered.

As to the explanation of these facts, Emmerich and Pawlowski come to very much the same conclusion. Apparently, with the exception of the pneumonia coccus, anthrax bacilli grow readily outside the body in cultivations containing also the other organisms mentioned, such as the erysipelas cocci. Hence the explanation cannot be that the erysipelas cocci *per se* prevented the growth of the anthrax bacilli in the body. It seems to be rather that these cocci irritate the cells of the body, the phagocytes, and increase their destructive power; it may be, as Emmerich suggests, that this irritation leads to a slight alteration in their physiological functions, so that they excrete some chemical substance which is very injurious to the anthrax bacilli.

How far these facts may be applied to the treatment of anthrax pustules in man, where, either from the situation or the size of the pustule, excision or cauterisation are impracticable, is a question very difficult to answer, and it seems to me that we must await the results of further investigations before any attempt to apply them practically in man would be justifiable. In any case, the facts are well worthy of note as affording another example of what unexpected factors may come into play if we once admit micro-organisms to wounds.

LOCAL AND SEASONAL CONDITIONS.

Lastly, we have certain local and seasonal conditions which appear in some way or other to influence the occurrence of some of these diseases. For example, Eschbaum, who has gone into this matter very carefully, finds that spontaneous erysipelas occurs most often apparently in February, then next most frequently in November, and least frequently in July. Apparently the cold months, and those where there is most moisture and greatest variations in temperature, show the greatest number of cases, and Eschbaum summarises the facts by saying that the cases are most numerous when we have marked variations of temperature, with a medium height of the barometer and a high degree of moisture. In the case of diphtheria also, cold and moisture seem to be a great predisposing cause, most cases occurring about the months of November and December. Kocher and Lücke have found that acute osteo-myelitis also is most frequent in winter. Probably, besides the seasonal conditions, the confinement in badly ventilated rooms, foul air and want of exercise, which come into play more frequently in cold and wet weather than in summer, have an important influence on the result. In the case of diseases of animals, more especially in the case of anthrax, there is a very marked relation between the season and the outbreaks of the epidemic, the disease apparently occurring where there is great moisture and high temperature. As regards anthrax, Chauveau has shown that increased atmospheric pressure tends to cause a loss of virulence.

As an example of the influence of locality on these suppurative diseases, we have the greater frequency of acute osteomyelitis in certain parts. For example this disease seems to be more frequent in Berne than anywhere else, and, according to Volkmann, it occurs next most frequently in Halle, and then in Marburg. These, however, are rather impressions than actual statistical facts.

Summary.

We thus come to the end of our considerations with regard to the factors involved in the production of suppuration and septic diseases. It must be admitted that our knowledge still shows many blanks, but nevertheless enough has been gained to enable us to judge what are the essential factors which come into play. That the pyogenic organisms are absolutely essential for the production of these diseases there can no longer be any doubt, but in many cases much depends on other conditions, of which the chief, probably, are the dose or number of the organisms and their concentration, general and local depression of vitality, and the seat of inoculation. If the organisms enter in large numbers sufficient to overcome the resistance of the body, they alone may cause the disease; usually, however, they enter in smaller numbers, and then other conditions become necessary in order to enable them to act. Of these conditions, the chief are, as I have said, depressed vitality, either local or general, combined with the possibility of their remaining in the weakened tissue. This depression of vitality may be brought about by conditions acting on the body generally, such as acute fevers; or by local conditions, more especially those which induce the early stage of inflammation, such as cold, injury, chemical substances, the products of the bacteria themselves, or the products of other kinds of bacteria which may happen to be growing along with them. Or again, the favourable condition may be some peculiarity in the soil as shown by variations in the character of the disease in accordance with the seat of inoculation and the anatomical arrangement of the part. The only factor, however, as I have said before, with which we can reckon with certainty, is the cocci themselves.

The whole matter is, as we have said, a battle between the tissues and the parasites, and may perhaps be best understood by comparing it with the warfare —especially with the sieges—of olden times. The opposing forces are, on the one hand, the bacteria, and, on the other hand, the body—the body representing the citadel, the cells of the body the garrison. Each of these forces has its own weapons. The weapons of the bacteria are, in the first place, poisonous substances which they throw into the body, and in the second place, starvation by with-drawing necessary materials from the body; the weapons of the body are less known, they are probably partly passive in the way of supplying bad food, and partly active in the production of ferments, in setting up digestive processes, and in withdrawing oxygen and other necessary substances from the parasites. If the parasites attack in large numbers and suddenly, they may carry the citadel before the guards—that is to say, the cells—become aware of their presence, and have time to turn their attention to the threatened part; or it may be in other cases they merely make a serious breach in the defences in which they can establish themselves, and from which they can send poisonous materials into the body, and gradually destroy it. If they are in too small numbers, they either fail to make their way into the body at all, or if they do get in, they cannot escape the guards, and are overpowered and destroyed. If the attack is only partially successful, the result is to irritate instead of destroying the defending agents, and these ulti-mately completely block the way or surround the parasites, which die and are cast out. This is seen in defensive inflammation, the object of which is to prevent the spread of the organisms by erecting a barrier through which the infective agents cannot pass ; in order to do this some tissue must be sacrificed in the neighbourhood of the bacteric deposit, just as it is sometimes necessary to pull down houses around a fire to prevent its spread. In the concurrent action of different species of bacteria, we have an example of warfare with allied forces. The new assistants may be of great value by their peculiar method of attack, taking the garrison unawares, for example, and thus admitting the other assail-ants. We have an example of this in the combined action of putrefactive and pyogenic bacteria, the putrefactive by their products weakening the tissues and breaking down their resistance, and thus enabling the others to enter. Or again, the reverse may be the case, and, like the erysipelas cocci and the anthrax bacilli, they may increase the power of the guards, or by greater vigour of growth they may crowd out the pathogenic organisms, while being themselves little, if at all, virulent.

I need not enter into details as to the pathology of all the various suppurative and septic diseases, it will be easy for anyone to apply the facts which have been stated to each disease, but in conclusion, I wish to make a few remarks with regard to the mode of entrance of these organisms into wounds.

Occurrence outside the Body.—These organisms are fairly widely distributed outside the body. In the air they have only been found on a very few occasions, and in very small numbers. The staphylococcus pyogenes aureus has been found on one or two occasions in the air of surgical wards, as has also the streptococcus of erysipelas. Experiments have been made as to the presence of the latter organism in the air of wards in which erysipelas patients were present, and they have, in one or two instances, been found in small numbers ; as a rule, however, they are apparently present only when the patients are con-valescent, and when desquamation of the skin is occurring, and it seems highly probable from the observations that have been made, that they are carried in the cutaneous scales thrown off during desquamation.

Eiselsberg exposed gelatine and agar plates in various parts of wards for a certain length of time. Colonies of different kinds of organisms were found ; in one instance staphylococcus pyogenes aureus. In a ward where there were four cases of erysipelas, one of which was convalescent, he obtained a development of streptococci on two occasions. On testing these organisms by cultivation and experiments on animals, he found that they were Fehleisen's erysipelas cocci. In an isolation ward in which there was a patient with erysipelas of the face, which was almost well and desquamating, and of the back, which was in full vigour, agar plates were exposed, one of them being placed close to the head of the patient. In the latter plate only did the streptococcus of erysipelas develop. In five cases Eiselsberg has also made cultivations with the cutaneous scales of patients suffering from erysipelas, and in four of the cases cultivations of the streptococcus have been obtained.

Erysipelas cocci have also been found in a post-mortem room, where cases of erysipelatous infection had occurred, and in this case the infection was supposed to have come from the floor. The pyogenic organisms are very rarely present in putrefying fluids, but they have been found on decomposing beef and in the water employed in kitchens for rinsing dishes. They are also sometimes present in the superficial layers of the soil. One of their most common seats outside the body is the skin, and they especially occur in parts where the skin is moist—for example, in the axillæ, between the nates, between the toes, &c.; they are also frequently present in connection with the hair and in the dirt beneath the nails. Fraenkel has found them in the secretions of the healthy pharynx, and Bockhardt found aureus and albus in large numbers in the nasal mucus of a patient suffering from chronic catarrh of the nose, and at the same time affected with sycosis of the upper lip.

Mode of Entrance into Wounds.—As regards the entrance of these organisms into wounds, they may get in during an operation from the air, from the instruments and hands of the operator or his assistants, from surrounding objects, or from the skin in the neighbourhood of the wound. We are now, however, sufficiently acquainted with the various precautions necessary to prevent the entrance of these organisms, and it is a comparatively easy matter to keep a wound made through a previously unbroken skin free from pyogenic organisms.

Although it is theoretically possible that in some cases these organisms might enter wounds from the blood in unhealthy subjects, I have never yet come across a case in which there was any ground for such a suspicion, nor where, when they were present, there was not a sufficient loophole for their penetration from without.

In the after treatment of wounds, there are two situations where the battle with these parasites takes place; it may either occur outside the wound, the organisms never being allowed to enter it, or it may take place inside the wound after their entrance has been permitted. It is hardly necessary to remark that in case of war we try to carry the war into the enemy's country; at all events, we do all we can by guarding the passes and borders, to prevent the enemy from entering our own country. And in like manner, in the case of wounds, it seems to me that it is much better to keep these pyogenic organisms out of the wounds, and to do battle with them outside the body, than to let them enter and trust to the efficacy of the tissues to repel their attacks. For, once they have entered the wound, it is but little that we can do to aid the action of the body, and what little we do has to be done with extreme caution, for not uncommonly our efforts, instead of being of service, cause a great deal of harm. As I have said, it is comparatively easy now to keep these pyogenic organisms out of a wound while it is being made, and to leave the wound without any of these microbes in it; the problem is to prevent their entrance afterwards. In this case, however, we have at any rate succeeded in transferring the field of battle from the interior of the wound to the surface of the body, and we have no longer to trust to the imperfect and but little understood action of the tissues; we can step in with vigorous action without any fear of doing harm. For it cannot be too much insisted on that antiseptic dressings are not in their essence applications to wounds; they are applications to the discharge which has come from the wound and to the skin around it.

The mode of entrance of these pyogenic cocci in cases of spontaneous acute abscesses, &c., is by no means clear in all cases. Where the abscesses occur in connection with lymphatic glands, there is no doubt that the organisms enter through wounds or inflamed patches on the cutaneous or mucous surface, are carried or grow along the lymphatic vessels, and are deposited in the lymphatic glands. In other cases, it is probable that the cocci are caught in the course of the lymphatic vessels, grow there, and set up an abscess. In other cases, the suppuration occurs directly beneath a wound or prick in the skin, the cocci simply spreading in the tissue or being carried by the juices of the part. Again, they may enter as the result of inunction through the glands of the skin, or through abraded epithelium, as is seen so often in the case of boils and pustules. I believe that if statistical facts could be obtained, it would be found that in by far the greatest number of cases, the infective material comes from without, either spreading directly into the tissue, or being carried along the lymphatics and deposited at various parts, and that the number of cases in which infection occurs from the blood is very small indeed. Where the infection occurs from the blood, the cocci reach the blood either from wounds or defects on the surface of the body, or from previous inflammatory deposits such as boils. I think it must be very seldom that these organisms enter through uninjured mucous membrane, though apparently in some cases no defect of the surface or inflamed area can be observed.

As to the mode of entrance of these pyogenic cocci after an operation, they may get in while the dressing is being changed, either by falling in from the air—though this must be of rare occurrence, seeing that they are so rarely present in the air — or by contamination by the surgeon's hands, instruments, &c., but this is also very easily avoided and ought not to occur; usually they spread in, either through the dressings or beneath them, in the intervals between the change of dressings. In my opinion, they most commonly spread in by growing in the discharge which is lying between the dressings and the skin, and in the superficial layers of the epidermis, more especially in the latter: for as the result of the irritation of the antiseptic employed, there is hypertrophy of the epithelium, and thus a large number of dead epithelial cells is present, which, being soaked with the discharge, form a good nidus for the development of the bacteria, unless, indeed, enough of the antiseptic has been communicated to the discharge and the epithelium from the dressing to render it an unsuitable soil for the growth of organisms. If this is not the case, the organisms will go on growing in the substance of this dead epithelium, protected by the superficial layers from the action of the dressing, and thus they may, if a dressing is left on for too long a time, ultimately reach the wound. This is not a mere theoretical speculation, for I have been able to trace the development of the organisms beneath the dressings from their margin towards the wound, the extent to which they spread varying with the length of time that the dressing has been applied. If these views as to the mode of entrance of bacteria into wounds are correct, it follows that it is very important, when a dressing is changed, to wash and thoroughly disinfect the skin around the wound as far as the dressing extended, and beyond it, with an antiseptic lotion, care being of course taken, by covering up the wound, not to infect it while so doing.   If this is done, then at each change of dressing the field of battle is transferred from the neighbourhood of the wound to the margin of the dressing, and, in accordance with the size of the dressing, this battlefield will be at a greater or less distance from the wound.

At the present time there are various kinds of dressings by which completely aseptic results can be obtained. I may mention the method which I now employ, and which for some time past has yielded uniformly good results.

The instruments are placed in 1-20 carbolic solution for half to one hour before the operation. This is quite sufficient to destroy the cocci present on them and most of the bacilli which may adhere to them are non-pathogenic in man, and cannot develop in healthy wounds. Besides, as the instruments are being constantly placed in 1-2000 sublimate solution during the operation, and the wounds are irrigated with sublimate solution, even the spores of the bacilli are destroyed. As a matter of fact, almost the only bacillus which we have to fear is the tubercle bacillus, and, therefore, if I have several operations to perform at one time, I always take the tubercular cases last, lest in using the same instruments (forceps, &c.) after they have become infected with tubercular material I should infect another wound.

The hands of the operator and his assistant are thoroughly disinfected with 1-20 carbolic lotion, and then with 1-2000 sublimate solution, a nail brush being freely used.

The skin in the neighbourhood of the seat of operation is thoroughly washed with 1-20 carbolic solution in which corrosive sublimate in the strength of 1-500 is dissolved. After wetting the skin with this solution I generally soap it, and then scrub it thoroughly with a nail brush, hairs being shaved off when present.

The sponges are kept permanently in 1-20 carbolic lotion, and washed in 1-2000 sublimate solution during the operation.

The operator has a basin of 1-2000 sublimate solution at hand, in which he frequently dips his instruments and hands during the course of the operation.

The parts (clothes, &c.) around the seat of operation are covered with towels wrung out of 1-2000 sublimate lotion.

No spray is employed, but the wound is irrigated from time to time, and constantly when stitching it up, with 1-2000 sublimate solution. In operations on joints and bones I irrigate the wound during the whole operation with 1-4000 sublimate solution.

As a dressing I apply first a large piece of carbolic gauze (about four layers in thickness), which is always kept in a jar of 1-2000 sublimate solution. Next a mass of alembroth gauze moistened, but not washed, in 1-2000 sublimate solution. (The reason for using the carbolic gauze is that if the alembroth gauze is applied next the skin it is apt to cause irritation, and even blistering of the skin, and to wash out the alembroth from the deeper layer of gauze, and thus to apply aseptic gauze not containing any store of the antiseptic next the skin is, I believe, a dangerous thing, for the sublimate from the outer part may not soak back into the discharge on the surface of the skin and into the superficial layer of epithelium in sufficient quantity to prevent the growth of micro-organisms.) Outside this I apply a large mass of salicylic wool which permits drying of the deeper parts, adds to the thickness of the dressing, and being less absorbent than the gauze, leads to the diffusion of the discharge throughout the gauze in the same manner as was formerly done by the mackintosh.

In some cases it is advisable to apply a narrow strip of protective over the line of union. I also use drainage tubes less frequently than formerly. In most cases where by moderate pressure the deeper parts of the wound can be kept in contact I do not use a drainage tube, but incorporate one or more large soft sponges with the dressing, and very often never change the dressing for ten or fourteen days, and then find the wound quite healed. A continuous suture of catgut applied like a button-hole stitch is often preferable to the interrupted suture.

There are a number of other materials which yield good results, and their number will probably be soon increased, but the method of dressing described yields, as I have said, uniform aseptic results, which leave nothing to be desired except greater simplicity.

I shall not enter any further into the subject of the treatment of wounds. We have now at our command a large number of antiseptics which more or less answer the purposes required, and it is only by careful attention to the exclusion of these organisms that we can obtain the best results. That we can completely exclude these bacteria from wounds, both at the operation and afterwards, I have been able to ascertain by numerous experiments and observations; and that just in proportion as we are successful in so doing we are to a like degree freed from the occurrence of suppuration and septic diseases, and can, to a like degree, reckon with confidence on rapid and painless healing of wounds with the least disturbance to the patient is a matter now of everyday observation.

LIST OF THE CHIEF PAPERS REFERRED TO IN
THE PRECEDING LECTURES.

ARLOING, CORNEVIN, and THOMAS, "Du Charbon bactérieu," Paris, 1883 ; and papers in Comptes Rendus, Revue de Méd., &c.

BABES, in Cornil and Babes, Les Bactéries, &c., Paris, 1886.

BAUMGARTEN'S Jahresbericht, vols. i. and ii. ; Lehrbuch der pathologischen Mykologie.

BECKER, Deutsche med. Wochenschrift, November 1883.

BERGMANN, Berliner klin. Wochenschrift, 1887, Nos. 1 and 2.

BIONDI, Deutsche med. Wochenschrift, 1886, No. 8.

BOCKHARDT, Monatshefte für praktische Dermatologie, No. 10, 1887.

BONOMÉ, Deutsche med. Wochenschrift, 1886.

BRIEGER, "Ueber Ptomaïne ;" Berliner klin. Wochenschrift, 1886 ; Fortschritte d. Med., No. 3, 1887.

BUMM, Archiv für Gynækologie, vols. xxiii., xxiv., and xxvii.; and Der Mikro-Organismus der gonorrhoischen Scheimhaut-Erkrankungen, Wiesbaden, 1887.

CHEYNE, Transactions of the Pathological Society, vol. xxx.; Brit. Med. Journal, 1883 and 1886 ; Antiseptic Surgery, London, 1882.

CORNIL, in Cornil and Babes, Les Bactéries, Paris, 1886.

COUNCILMAN, Virchow's Archiv, vol. xcii.

EISELSBERG, Von Langenbeck's Archiv, vol. xxxv.

EMMERICH, Fortschritte d. Med., vol. v., 1887.

EMMERICH and MATTEI, Fortschritte d. Med., vol. v., 1887.

ERNST, Ueber die pyogenen Wirkungen des Staphylococcus pyogenes aureus. Würzburg, 1886.

ESCHBAUM, Beiträge zur Statistik einiger acut entzündlichen und Infectionskrankheiten, Bonn, 1880.

ESCHERICH, Münchener med. Wochenschrift; Fortschritte d. Med., vol. iii.

FEHLEISEN, Aetiologie d. Erysipels, Berlin, 1883; and also Microorganisms in Disease, New Syd. Society, 1886.

FRAENKEL, A., Deutsche med. Wochenschrift, 1884 and 1885; Zeitschrift für klin. Med., vol. x., 1886.

FRAENKEL and FREUDENBERG, Centralblatt f. klin. Med., 1885.

CARRÉ, Fortschritte d. Med., 1885 and 1886.

GRAWITZ, Virchow's Archiv, vols. cviii. and cx.; Charité-Annalen, vol. xi.

GRAWITZ and DE BARY, Virchow's Archiv, vol. cviii.

HAJEK, Centralblatt f. Bacteriologie, vol. i., 1887.

HAUSER, Faülniss Bakterien.

HEUBNER, Die experimentelle Diphtherie, Leipzig, 1883.

HOFFA, Fortschritte d. Med., 1886, No. 3.

HOLMFELD, CHRISTMAS-DIRKINCK-, Fortschritte d. Med., No. 13, 1887.

HUBER, Virchow's Archiv, vol. cvi.

HUEPPE, Berliner klin. Wochenschrift, 1887.

KAMMERER, Centralblatt f. Chirurgie, 1884.

KITT, Centralblatt f. Bacteriologie, vol. i., 1887 ; Fortschritte d. Med., No. 5, 1886.

KLEMPERER, Zeitschrift f. klin. Med., vol. xi. 1886.

KNAPP, Archiv für Augenheilkunde by Knapp and Schweigger, 1886.

KOCH, "Traumatic Infective Diseases," New Sydenham Society.

KOCHER, Deutsche Zeitschr. f. Chirurgie, vol. xi., 1879.

KRASKE, Berliner klin. Wochenschrift, 1886 ; Langenbeck's Archiv, vol. xxxiv.

KRAUSE, Fortschritte d. Med., vol. ii., 1884.

LASSAR, Virchow's Archiv.

LANDERER, Volkmann's Sammlung, No. 259, 1885.

LISTER, Trans. Royal Soc., 1858.

LOEFFLER, Mittheilungen aus. d. k. Gesundheitsamte, vol. ii.

METSCHNIKOFF, Virchow's Archiv, vol. cvii.

NEISSER, Centralblatt, f. d. med., Wiss. 1879, No. 28.

OGSTON, Brit. Med. Journal, 1881 ; Journal of Anat. and Physiol., vols. xvi. and xvii., 1882.

ORTHMANN, Virchow's Archiv, vol. xc.

PASSET, Fortschritte d. Med. 1885, Nos. 2 and 3 ; Untersuchungen ueber die eiterigen Phlegmone des Menschen, Berlin, 1885.

PAWLOWSKY, Virchow's Archiv, vol. cviii.

RIBBERT, Deutsche med. Wochenschrift, 1884 and 1885 ; Fortschritte d. Med., 1886, No. 1.

RINNE, Centralblatt f. Bakteriologie, vol. ii., No. 19, 1887.

ROSENBACH, Mikro-Organismen bei d. Wund-Infections-Krankheiten des Menschen, Wiesbaden, 1884 ; Deutsche Zeitsch. f. Chir., vol. x. Deutsche med. Wochenschrift, 1884.

RUIJS, Deutsche med. Wochenschrift, 1885.

SCHEUERLEN, Langenbeck's Archiv, vol. xxxii. ; Fortschritte d. Med., 1887.

STRAUS, Société de Biologie, 1884.

UFFREDUZZI, Fortschritte d. Med, No. 5, 1886.

WEGNER, Langenbeck's Archiv, 1877.

WOLLENBERG, Die Lehre von der acuten, infect. Osteomyelitis. Inaug. Diss., Halle, 1885.

WYSSOKOWITSCH, Zeitschrift für Hygiene, vol. i., No. 1 ; Virchow's Archiv, vol. ciii.

ZUCKERMANN, Centralblatt f. Bakteriologie, vol. i., No. 17.

INDEX.

G

INDEX.

.

www.ingramcontent.com/pod-product-compliance
Lightning Source LLC
Chambersburg PA
CBHW030629270326
41927CB00007B/1363